Penguin Education X35
Penguin Science of Behaviour
General Editor: B. M. Foss

Clinical Psychology
Editor: Graham A. Foulds

Disorders of Memory and Learning
George A. Talland

Disorders of Memory and Learning

George A. Talland

Penguin Books

Penguin Books Ltd, Harmondsworth,
Middlesex, England
Penguin Books Inc., 7110 Ambassador Road,
Baltimore, Md 21207, U.S.A.
Penguin Books Australia Ltd, Ringwood,
Victoria, Australia

First published 1968
Copyright © the Estate of G. A. Talland, 1968

Made and printed in Great Britain by
Hazell Watson & Viney Ltd,
Aylesbury, Bucks
Set in Linotype Plantin

Penguin Science of Behaviour

This book is one of the first in an ambitious project, the *Penguin Science of Behaviour*, which will cover a very wide range of psychological inquiry. Many of the short 'unit' texts will be on central teaching topics, while others will deal with present theoretical and empirical work which the Editors consider to be important new contributions to psychology. We have kept in mind both the teaching divisions of psychology and also the needs of psychologists at work. For readers working with children, for example, some of the units in the field of Developmental Psychology will deal with techniques in testing children, other units will deal with work on cognitive growth. For academic psychologists, there will be units in well-established areas such as Learning and Perception, but also units which do not fall neatly under any one heading, or which are thought of as 'applied', but which nevertheless are highly relevant to psychology as a whole.

The project is published in short units for two main reasons. Firstly, a large range of short texts at inexpensive prices gives the teacher a flexibility in planning his course and recommending texts for it. Secondly, the pace at which important new work is published requires the project to be adaptable. Our plan allows a unit to be revised or a fresh unit to be added with maximum speed and minimal cost to the reader.

Above all, for students, the different viewpoints of many authors, sometimes overlapping, sometimes in contradiction, and the range of topics Editors have selected will reveal the complexity and diversity which exist beyond the necessarily conventional headings of an introductory course.

B.M.F.

Contents

Editorial Foreword

The author makes his standpoint clear in his Preface. He has found very limited use for paradigms in animal learning, in rote learning generally and in stimulus-response psychology. Here, as in his distinctions between reconstruction and reproduction, between amnesias and apraxias, agnosias, etc., between disordered function and temporary lapses, his judgements, undogmatic and relaxed, mark out an author who has arrived at his position after careful thought and experimentation. Thus : 'Occasional failures in recall or a temporary difficulty in learning need not be taken as symptomatic of a disorder in a function. ... Every so often one's performance can exceed as well as fall short of those mean values that correspond to the bulk of one's efforts and achievements. We infer a disorder from a permanent or extensive disability in comparison with previous performance or in comparison with a suitably defined control group.' These occasional failures and distortions of recall are vividly discussed and illustrated in the early chapters. In the later chapters Dr Talland turns to the permanent or extensive disabilities. By the end we have been helped to appreciate that, though a useful distinction can be made between disorders and temporary lapses, there are aspects which are relatively continuous as well as aspects which are relatively discontinuous.

The chapter on 'Biological Models of Memory and Learning' should prove of especial value, particularly to those psychologists who have come to the subject from a more social wing.

This book was written when the author knew that he was dying of cancer. The lucid organization, the concise, sensitive and often humorous style cannot fail to draw the admiration of any reader, both for the man and the scholar. After I had received the completed manuscript and suggested that he might expand certain parts, particularly his own work on the Korsakoff psychosis, he wrote to say that I had caught him at a bad time and he regretted that my suggestion could not be followed. Within two months George Talland was dead. He refers to only two of his sixty-odd publications. Those who share my regret that he was unable to meet my suggestion that he should treat his own work in greater detail will find this done in his book *Deranged Memory: A Psychonomic Study of the Amnesic Syndrome* (Academic Press, 1965).

G.A.F.

Preface

This book was written to form part of a series in clinical psychology, and its primary subject is the disorders of memory and learning observed in psychiatric and neurological illness. Rather than present these disorders as quaint aberrations and irrational curiosities, I have attempted to analyse them in relation to normal learning and memory function, and in order to do that I have had to outline some principles of normal learning and remembering before delving deep into the pathology of these functions.

I believe that topics familiar from clinical psychology cannot be understood properly without some foundations in general psychology. My belief does not imply that the discovery of the laws and mechanisms of normal function necessarily precedes our observations of abnormal function. Indeed, we owe a large portion of our knowledge of learning and remembering to clinical studies. Not a few of these studies are quite spectacular and of such immediate interest to the general reader, as well as to the trained psychologist, that they provide an apparently inexhaustible source of themes for novelists and playwrights. A catalogue of case reports – clinical and fictional – of amnesias, multiple personalities, fugue states, etc., would undoubtedly make entertaining reading, but it would hardly amount to a systematic statement of our knowledge of these mental disturbances. That goal is more likely to be attained by eschewing the spectacular or giving it no more than its due weight, and examining the commonplace examples of deranged function and the residual processes of normal function as well.

The general plan of this book follows my own ideas of what comes first, what second, as well as certain outlines common to the series. The latter dictated a classification according to diagnostic classes, even though symptoms may cut across the boundaries so established. Chapter 1 is devoted to a definition of the subject matter indicated by the title, as I understand it. Chapters 2 and 3 discuss psychological theories of learning and remembering, and of the processes that, according to the more elaborate theories, constitute human learning and memory. Chapter 4 summarizes some current biological theories that have been influenced by clinical observations of memory disorders, and in turn have influenced the thought of psychologists. Chapters 5 and 6 present clinical examples of disorders in memory and learning and of other related abnormalities, according to the nosological categories of psychiatry and neurology. Chapter 7 treats the same material, with different examples and from the point of view of the dysfunction regardless of its aetiology. Chapter 8 surveys some of the tests in current use to assess clinical impairments of memory and learning, and the few techniques available to restore defective function.

My theoretical position differs in certain basic premises sufficiently from that held by many other psychologists to warrant a summary statement. I do not dispute that some examples of human learning have many essential features in common with the type of learning animals display, for example in a conditioning experiment, but I believe that those examples are not very representative of human learning and remembering, and even less informative about the disorders that can be observed in human learning and memory function. By the same token, I can find only limited use for paradigms in rote learning, even though they may involve verbal symbols. The vast majority of disorders in human learning and memory are not observable in firmly established habits, that is in learning acquired rote fashion, but in the unavailability of specific memories or in their distortion and contextual misplacement. These disabilities, whether temporary or permanent, point to defects in the operations by which information is filed for future reference, stored, and extracted from the records on demand.

The occasions on which failures of learning or memory became manifest in the clinical setting may resemble the experimental situation in which a stimulus is presented to elicit a response – and the response does not follow. It would be a serious mistake, though, to conclude from this that intact learning or remembering therefore fits the stimulus–response paradigm. Except in a metaphorical sense, human behaviour does not include a great deal that is a response to anything that can be termed a stimulus but is determined by spontaneously initiated action programmes. The planning and execution of such programmes is, of course, closely dependent on an intact memory function, and the more severely impaired this is, the more behaviour approximates a purely respondent model. If my occasional use of the word 'response' should contradict this statement, let me plead the necessity of complying with current technical terminology. I have at least tried to avoid using the ambiguous term 'stimulus', except when treating of theories that are founded on this concept.

Any discussion of memory or learning must resort to a number of hypothetical constructs if it attempts more than a quantitative account of performance. Those in current usage have been borrowed from several diverse sources and most of these terms are sufficiently close to their meaning in non-technical speech to be understood; in some instances, however, a definition seemed to be desirable. If this book succeeds in conveying to the reader my ideas on the topics discussed, he and I will be greatly indebted to my wife, Non, for her advice on rephrasing certain passages, as well as to Drs Frank Ervin, John Garcia, Michael McGuire and Nancy Waugh, who have read the first manuscript and whose comments and suggestions have been incorporated in the present version.

George A. Talland
1967

1 Introduction: Memory, Learning and Disordered Function

In the psychiatric literature there is a well-documented report of an epileptic patient, a virtually illiterate man, who one day under seizure preached a funeral sermon in Latin. It was a sermon that he could never have heard in full but must have put together from snatches overheard on several occasions, presumably under similarly abnormal conditions. After the seizure cleared up he remembered nothing of his performance, could neither reconstruct nor indeed understand any of the Latin text, and also failed to respond with the appropriate religiously tinged words in a word association test. Hypnotic experiments elicited no more material than did questions and tests under normal conditions of wakefulness. Another report tells of an idiot who, in a fit of anger, recounted a complicated incident that he had witnessed long before and which at the time seemed to make no impression on him.

These are undoubtedly examples of disordered memory, although much less common than those of everyday forgetting, yet hardly more difficult to explain. We would not call them disorders of learning even though they do exemplify some anomalies in learning. Speakers of English use both these terms, memory and learning, with confidence and they rarely fail to communicate their intended meaning. Many biologists and engineers cite them with no less assurance, assigning to each term a very special meaning which does not quite correspond to common usage. Quite a few psychologists refer to learning and memory in a firm belief that these processes are sufficiently defined by their manifestations in certain performance tests, and that all their varieties can be reduced to one or a few basic types. Other psychologists are inclined to use both terms with some reservations, for they believe that learning and memory refer to complex processes that vary in their composition and are not fully understood.

The traditional distinction between habits manifested in action and memories vested in ideation plays no part in a behaviourally oriented psychology. Memories turn into habits by attaining autonomy, and to ask at what precise moment this happens is, as Delay (1942) remarked, as pointless as to ask how many swallows are necessary to herald the arrival of spring. Learning, of course, applies alike to the acquisition of habits and of the contents of memories, and indeed behaviourist psychology has dealt with the laws and problems of remembering and forgetting under the head of learning. Recent interest in 'short-term memory' is an outgrowth of learning theory and experiments. Melton (1963), one of the leading spokesmen of this currently thriving activity in psychology, regards the subject-matter of learning and of memory as identical; one is concerned with the change observed between one trial and the next, the other with the interval between the same two trials. This is the position of experimenters working in the tradition of Ebbinghaus (1885) who laid the foundations of laboratory research in verbal learning.

Clinical investigators of memory disorders are more inclined to distinguish between processes and mechanisms of learning and of remembering and, while primarily interested in defects of the acquisition and application of verbally coded information, are unlikely to concur with Underwood's statement that 'rote verbal learning is central to all human learning' (1949). The laws established in laboratory studies should indeed be considered and tested in systematic analyses of learning and memory disorders but ought to be given preference only if they offer the most parsimonious or comprehensive explanation. They apply to one type of learning and their relevance to other types of learning cannot be taken for granted but must be demonstrated empirically.

Memory: Reconstruction or Reproduction

Memory belongs to a single organism, man or animal. I cannot remember your thoughts or experiences although I can learn about them and remember what I have learnt. The politician's, historian's, or biologist's references to national or racial or other collective memories is suspect and accepted at best as a metaphor or as a statistical construct. Nowadays, however, we hear quite a lot about the memory of machines, of computers; and the manner in which these electronic instruments function has suggested new hypotheses to students of human memory. Computer memories can be disordered and, superficially at least, disordered in much the same way as human memory.

Geneticists talk about memory when they refer to constitutional or functional patterns transmitted from one generation to the next. They have indeed discovered the mechanism and code by which this transmission proceeds, an achievement of immense significance in its own right but also in indicating a model of the mechanisms by which information acquired since birth might be coded and stored. Their model fits the mechanism by which one type of life experience is 'remembered', that is the highly selective production of antibodies, and its applicability may also extend to quite different examples of information storage. Its focus is on coding devices for storage – on memories rather than remembering. Remembering is a constructive process, not mere duplication, and memory disorders can arise from other defects than the erasure of a neurally coded record. Obvious examples in point are the later recovery of some memory that seems lost on a previous occasion, the embellishment and distortion of observations, and the confounding or fusion of separate incidents.

Even those who view memory as a purely reproductive function do not in fact behave strictly according to their tenet. If they ask you for a full account of a trip you have

just completed, they too will expect you to condense and
edit the information collected. If you trace your way
through a town you have not seen these last thirty years
they will applaud you for 'remembering' your bearings
amidst all the unfamiliar landmarks and will accord you
scant credit for halting at the first juncture that looks unfamiliar. Examples of exact replication are probably even
rarer in motor than in verbal behaviour. Poetry and some
prose is learned with the purpose of literal reproduction,
so are legal formulas, the liturgy and magic incantations.
The supernatural powers are feared to be exacting; the
slightest deviation from the sacred text may arouse their
anger or lose its propitiating efficacy. Man is more
tolerant and only has himself to blame for all the annoy-
ance he courts by demanding exact reproduction in recall.

Small lapses in memory, even if noticed, are not regarded as disorders; generally one allows a fair latitude for
errors in fact, in detail and in contextual placement. An
artistic recreation of the past, although it may amount to
a sustained exercise in self-deception or in deliberate falsi-
fication, hardly qualifies for a disorder of memory. The
forgetfulness of mundane matters of the scholar, absorbed
in his speculations and even the broken appointments of
those with much flimsier claims to preoccupation are
accepted and explained without any suspicion of memory
disorder. The implication is that the absent-minded professor or the scatter-brained adolescent could remember
all that they should if they but tried. Only when con-
centrated effort fails to retrieve information that was
readily available before, and especially data relating to
personal experiences, are we prepared to attribute the
defect to a memory disorder.

Errors in testimony

In certain types of ostensibly factual reporting, we must
take it for granted that a large proportion of the details
will be incorrect, even though presented with the utmost
certitude and in good faith. Victims of assault are

notoriously unreliable witnesses regarding the description of their assailants, but then so are onlookers who watched in safety. An event need not stir up any affect in order to be grossly misrepresented in recollection. Stern (1938), who carried out some revealing experiments on testimony, once arranged that during a lecture a strange man should walk into the class and ask for permission to look at a book in the adjoining library. After reading for a short while, he walked out with the book under his arm, contrary to regulations. The members of the class, who watched these proceedings with little or no interest, were unexpectedly asked a week later to report the incident and describe the man. Far from refusing to respond on the grounds of imperfect observation or recollection they all volunteered to supply a report and tended to give it in detail and at length. Most of their statements were incorrect, so that no judge could have reconstructed an accurate image 'from the contradictory statements as to the dress and appearance of the man and as to whether or not he wore glasses'. Only a small minority of the respondents reported that the man had walked out with the book, some abstained from answering the question and the majority stated that he had put it back on the shelves.

Stern was of the opinion that the majority declared this without thinking, whereas it is more likely that their incorrect report was precisely the product of their thinking and their reconstruction of the episode from a rule they knew, having failed to observe its breach in this instance. Commenting on the results of other experiments, Stern showed how much more false recollection is elicited by cross questioning than in free recall, and that children and adolescents, when asked to describe a picture immediately after its inspection, gave false positive answers to one out of every four catch questions.

The remarkable features of these testimonies are the witness's readiness to respond and his self-confidence when in fact he ought to be cautious and hedge his statements. That quite substantive factual errors can occur in

testimony based, not on casual observation, but on deliberately rehearsed information is apparent from a court case
reported by Somerville (1931). A young man telephoned
the police that his mother had shot herself; the ambulance duly arrived and took her to the hospital, where the
son left her while she was still unconscious. After she had
regained consciousness, the woman gave a lucid account
of the circumstances that had preceded the accident. She
said that she had been writing a letter, correctly naming
the person to whom she had written, that her son had
been standing beside her and that she had told him 'Go
away, Donald, and don't annoy me.' Then there was
something like a pistol shot, implying if not explicitly
stating that the son had shot her. Subsequently the
woman developed septic meningitis, became delirious and
died. On the strength of her statements the son was duly
charged with matricide.

In the trial the crucial evidence was given by Professor
Robertson and was based on one of Dr Somerville's cases.
This concerned a cyclist who had been knocked down on
the road by another cyclist. He was unconscious when Dr
Somerville arrived on the scene on his motor cycle a few
minutes later, but recovered in the course of the medical
examination. Next day the patient stated and clearly believed that the accident had been caused by the doctor
running into him and he continued in that belief even
though it was contradicted by the man who had actually
collided with him. The cyclist exemplified a situation in
which a head injury resulted in the deletion of a segment
from a person's memory without concomitant confusion
regarding the preceding or subsequent events. Professor
Robertson's testimony rested on the analogy of this
example and of the confusion shown by the defendant's
mother following her injury.

The cyclist's case illustrated the process by which experiences separated by a relatively long gap of unconsciousness are tied closely together in recall and it helped
to clear the defendant of the charge brought against him.

The fact that his mother appears to have been completely
oblivious of her intent to commit suicide is not unique
either; a similar example is quoted in the discussion that
followed Dr Somerville's presentation. These findings are
of considerable interest in regard to memory disorders
associated with brain injury, but the reason for sum-
marizing the two cases at this point is a remarkable distortion of the facts reported by Professor Robertson in the
witness box. Although he had twice checked the details of
the road accident with Dr Somerville, he described it as
one between two motor cycles and spoke of Dr Somerville
as arriving in his car. He also gratuitously commented that,
as a result of the cyclist's false report, 'matters became
strained between' his parents and the doctor, whereas all
that Dr Somerville said was that they had looked
strangely at him when he visited the patient the day after
the accident.

Varieties of Learning

Whatever can be remembered can also be forgotten but
not all that can be learned is subject to forgetting, or
indeed to remembering. There is a wide area of overlap
between learning and remembering, and that includes
skills, trades, lessons and all the subject matter of formal
instruction. Psychologists generally also treat the acquisition and development of habits, traits, attitudes and
opinions as learning processes. These are not forgotten but
are subject to disuse or reversal, to alteration and extinction. Whether the manner in which such changes occur
also explains how information is forgotten is a matter of
theoretical interest but, whatever the outcome, common
usage is likely to preserve the distinction between learning and remembering; denoting processes of acquisition
with the one and those of recall, recognition, and re-
application with the other.

The infant's behavioural repertoire expands steadily
from the day of birth. This expansion continues well into

the adult years and normally throughout the entire life span, although in later years at a markedly reduced rate and against compensatory restrictions. A small contribution to this process can be attributed entirely to maturation; the remainder is added, developed and perfected by learning. The scope for learning, although wide, is still limited by our biological equipment. Certain orders of physical events are as definitely beyond the range of man's sensory capacities as the skills of flying or surviving under water without mechanical aids. Reflexes and instincts are examples of genetically determined, that is unlearned, behaviour but the manifestation of instincts is very considerably subject to learning and so are the occasions when some reflexes are triggered off. We all learn to blush on certain occasions, although we do not have to learn each appropriate occasion separately.

Maladaptive learning

Blushing, perhaps a trivial example, is worth considering for two reasons. Firstly, the child learns to activate a physiological response in certain social situations, to a class of symbols, even though this response offers him neither escape nor any reward, and he will continue to make this response under similar circumstances for the rest of his life. Secondly, he does not learn a complete list of situations, or an exhaustive inventory of the words and phrases that elicit a blush; he learns rules by which he can generalize. The rules he learns may not be universally valid. They may be limited to a culture or sub-culture, but even within those confines their observation is more likely to cause him distress than pleasure. Nevertheless, he only rarely – if ever – succeeds in ridding himself of this troublesome learned response.

Blushing is a mild example of maladaptive learning and, because it is so common, it is not regarded as a disorder. Other examples of maladaptive physiological responses that are both less common and more crippling, such as asthma, have been considered in this light, but probably this sort of categorizing carries more conviction when it is applied to behaviour that seems to be more fully under the person's control, such as nail-biting or the avoidance of confined spaces. It seems fairly obvious that those morbid habits were acquired in ways quite similar to such eminently laudable habits as brushing one's teeth and avoiding disreputable dives.

Behaviour disorders are thus very largely learning disorders. This statement does not minimize the influence of hereditary disposition, of social norms and settings, or of such important life experiences as arise from interpersonal relationships, diseases and accidents. Those conditions set limits to what can be learned and some of them also furnish the content of learning. It seems likely that a man who has difficulties with authority figures derives his problems very considerably from some threatening interpersonal relationships in his own experience. It is also quite probable that given a different genetic constitution he would have reacted to those experiences in a different manner or that a chronic infirmity would aggravate his troubles. Insofar as his problems remain unrelieved in the face of objectively favourable experiences, they present an example of a learning disorder.

A definition of learning disorders that comprises the various types and symptoms of personality maladjustment and mental illness is, however, too wide for the purposes of this book. It is concerned primarily with disturbances in the acquisition and reproduction of verbally coded information and, to a lesser extent, of motor skills. Both these types of learning have been extensively investigated in the experimental laboratory and there is a vast literature analysing the performance of human as well as animal subjects. The method for verbal material is principally rote or paired-associate learning which allows for a controlled investigation of certain factors that determine the acquisition and reproduction of information, but represents a limiting rather than a typical instance of verbal learning. Some experiments in skill learning seem to be more informative about the processes and defects in verbal function – as well as in human problem solving and concept formation – than the standard rote learning techniques.

Disordered Function

Occasional failures in recall or a temporary difficulty in learning need not be taken as symptomatic of a disorder in a function. All our functions are exercised within limits and, with such heterogeneous and often complex functions as remembering and learning, the limits are wide. Every so often one's performance can exceed as well as fall short of those mean values that correspond to the bulk of one's efforts and achievements. We infer a disorder from a permanent or extensive disability in comparison with previous performance or in comparison with a suitably defined control group. Any attempt to remedy such a disorder presupposes its ascertainment and definition, if possible in terms of impaired processes as well as of performance defects.

Structural and functional damage

As in other areas of abnormal psychology, there is an established usage that distinguishes organic and functional disorders of learning and memory. This distinction is derived from an obsolete metaphysical position which regards man, if not other animate creatures, as constituted of a dual substance, body and mind. Behavioural defects attributable to bodily damage are called organic, similar or other defects observed without concomitant neural disorders are called functional. Implicitly, such a distinction is based on the postulate that anomalies manifested in organic function can originate in or are caused by some non-organic agency; it also suggests that the term 'organic function' entails a contradiction.

In fact the distinction only reflects our insufficient knowledge of cerebral mechanisms and of structural defects in the brain in normal as well as in deranged function. Organic disorders mean behavioural defects associated with known structural damage of the brain; functional disorders are similar or different defects observed in behaviour when the limited techniques available cannot show a corresponding impairment in the brain. Since nowadays there is fairly universal agreement that the organ of the mind is the brain, it follows that disorders in mental function, for example in learning and in remembering, must reflect disorders in brain function. All mental disorders are organic as well as functional, and the only debatable point is whether the organic damage is structural. Theoretically, brain function could be disordered with completely intact tissue, for example, as a result of some disturbance in the map, or rate, or intensity of neural transmission.

A closely related distinction of mental disturbances that can involve memory and learning defects is that between neurological and psychiatric diseases, or between neurogenic – a term rarely used because of a preference for organic – and psychogenic disorders. The former include derangements in mental functions that can be directly attributed to brain lesions, mechanical shocks and other physical traumata, toxaemias, tumours and inflammations in cerebral tissue. Psychogenic disorders are those attributed by inference as well as by direct observation to emotional shocks and stresses. Certain personality types are more prone than others to develop psychogenic disorders under objectively similar stresses, while vulnerability to neurogenic diseases varies little within an age group. The distinction between these two types of mental disturbances is in terms of their aetiology; their symptoms and signs are often identical and the conditions that immediately result in a neurogenic disorder can also provide occasions for the emergence of psychogenic diseases – typically as a secondary or delayed effect.

2 Acquisition of Habits, Skills and Information

Learning

Learning has traditionally been viewed as the establishment of new associations. This paradigm satisfies most psychologists as long as it admits sufficient complexity in the patterning of the associations. Its shortcomings are most apparent when it is formulated in its simplest version, as an association between a closely defined stimulus (S) and an equally isolated and standardized response (R), without regard to neurological processes or psychological functions evolved in the course of past experience that intervene between S and R. The S–R model owes its appeal to its simplicity and so does the experimental technique of conditioning which is customarily, if somewhat cavalierly, credited with satisfying the requirements of a pure S–R model.

Conditioning

Conditioning certainly represents one type of learning as this term is defined by psychologists, and more probably several types of learning. As a technique it stems from a physiological laboratory and, according to some weighty opinions, conditioning as formulated by Pavlov (1927) accounts only for enduring changes in the function of the autonomic nervous system. Pavlov's first interest was the physiology of the digestive glands and he discovered the conditioned response when he observed that his dogs would begin to salivate at the sound of the bell that heralded feeding time even before the food came into their sight.

Salivation when food is in an animal's mouth is an inborn, unlearnt response; salivation at the sight of the food or at the sound of a signal that regularly precedes it is a learnt response. Pavlov explained this learning as a transfer of the response from the unconditional (US) to the conditional stimulus (CS). The mechanism of this learning process was the regular contiguity between the two stimuli; the conditioned response, that is salivation on hearing the bell, in no way influenced the desired objective which was the arrival of food. In order for conditioning to occur it was necessary not only that the food be chewed but also that the dog enter the situation after hours of food deprivation. If, following conditioning, there were several trials in which no food arrived after the bell, the conditioned response would extinguish. *Extinction* implies the disappearance of a learned behaviour but not its unavailability, since an extinguished response can be restored not only by reinforced trials but is apt to recover spontaneously after a while. Extinction is thus a highly functional type of forgetting, rather like an additional learning process, that is, learning not to respond.

Pavlovian conditioning of human subjects typically follows a somewhat different design from reinforcing a positive response by a reward. Experimental examples are those of hand withdrawal or eyelid closure to some originally neutral stimulus that is paired with electric shock in the one instance, with an airpuff in the other. One of the best known examples is the case of little Albert, the eleven-month-old boy who was conditioned to fear rabbits and fur as well as his pet white rat. To begin with Albert was fond of playing with his rat, but then every time he touched it he heard the noise of a hammer banging against an iron bar. After a number of occasions that paired this frightening sound with the pet animal Albert, who was always scared by the one, came to fear the other and for good measure all kinds of other furry objects as well (Watson and Rayner, 1920).

Learning of symptoms

This experiment in emotional conditioning may indeed

serve as a learning prototype of phobias and possibly of other neurotic symptoms. Some convincing arguments have been put forward for treating behavioural or emotional disorders as the products of Pavlovian conditioning and thus to account for their persistence in spite of their maladaptive function. By the same token, therapies designed on the conditioning model have been used to relieve patients of their symptoms. It is certainly true that some neurotic symptoms, anxieties and phobias in particular, are as irrationally related to the causal connexions in the patient's life situation as the typical conditioned stimulus, such as bells, tuning forks, hinged bars and electrically charged grids, to that of the experimental animal. The analogy serves well enough for reconstructing the processes by which the maladjustive learning may have occurred, but hardly for its prediction or effective prevention. To conclude that little Albert has transferred his fear from a nasty sound to a white rat, and then generalized it to other furry things, begs the question of why he abstracted the furry quality of his pet of all its many equally irrelevant attributes.

Pavlov was also a pioneer in producing an experimental neurosis by demanding of his dogs increasingly difficult perceptual discriminations in order to make the appropriate conditioned response. After prolonged training under those conditions the animal's orderly behaviour broke down and gave way to manifestations of violence, all unrelated to any consummatory goal, and persisting even after the dog was released from the experimental harness. Pavlov recognized this behaviour as analogous to the acute neuroses of patients and attributed it to a conflict of excitatory and inhibitory processes in the brain. Other dogs manifested their experimental neurosis by different types of behavioural anomalies, a variability Pavlov attributed to differences in the relative strength, mobility and equilibrium of the two antagonistic cortical processes.

The reflex model of learning

Excitation and inhibition in Pavlov's scheme were hypothetical processes within the brain that he invoked in order to provide a physiological foundation for his behavioural observations. They were conceived on the pattern of actual physiological observations, more especially of Sherrington's (1906) model of the spinal reflexes, but not on any direct observation of brain function. Pavlov's typology and model of learning are psychological theories for all their ostensible neurophysiological formulation, and have been modified and elaborated by students of behaviour to account for behaviour which, whether simple or complex, does not fit the hypothetical model of the reflex arc or even of a chain of reflexes.

As has been pointed out earlier, the great virtue of the conditioning experiment is its simplicity, which also allows for rigorous control of its component factors. The few examples listed above all exemplify the basic pattern of transferring an innate response – physiological, skeletal or affective – to some stimulus that would not elicit it prior to this learning experience. Albert's pathetic story also illustrates the range of generalization in conditioning, a potentiality that experiments in higher-order conditioning have exploited more methodically. Criticisms regarding the inadequacy of Pavlov's conditioning paradigm are based not so much on the limitations of the process as on the limitations imposed by the basic elements on which the process can be built.

Associative learning

No matter how rigid the behavioural repertoire of some animal species, man's is much more varied than can be derived from such stereotyped innate S–R connexions as, for example, food eliciting salivation or noxious stimuli prompting withdrawal. Moreover, a breakdown of behaviour into stereotyped responses or movements may offer advantages for its analysis but it violates the principles by which complex organisms actually behave. These are the combination and sequencing of any pattern of responses or movements that achieve the goal, whether this be the acquisition or avoidance of an object. Animals, like people, learn how to obtain or avoid something, not an invariant sequence of movements; if that is what they learn, we call it *fixation* and recognize it as a sign of mal-adjustment or neurosis. Learning is manifested as much in the capacity to vary behaviour in accordance with the situation as in the capacity to reproduce it.

A learnt response is any member of a class of responses defined by functional equivalence; it is not genetically fixed and neither is the stimulus. To disentangle a stimulus from the environment involves perceptual differentiation and categorization on a functional principle, that is previous learning. Apart from the limited array of innate sensori-motor connexions, such perceptual learning must precede conditioning and also another important technique of learning, that is, imitation. Nor is contiguity, even in combination with reinforcement, a sufficient condition of connecting a response with a stimulus. There is a degree of specificity built into the organism. As Garcia and Ervin (1967) have shown, rats will avoid food they had ingested prior to the intravenous administration of a nauseating agent – even with an interval of one hour, that is, far in excess of the longest temporal gap between con-ditional and unconditional stimulus recognized by condi-tioning theory – but will not avoid the site associated with feeding, injection and nausea. By the same token, they will avoid the spot where they were given a painful electric shock but not the food they received prior to that ex-perience. Furthermore, given the choice between a small food pellet to eat and a large pellet of the same desirable food followed by a shock, they quickly learn to pick the large pellet and to eat it on that side of the box that holds the small pellet and where the floor is not electrified.

Instrumental conditioning

The first objection to the Pavlovian theory has been met by operant conditioning. Skinner (1938), who originated this technique, distinguished two kinds of response: those elicited by specific stimuli and the 'operant' which enters into an S–R connexion only after conditioning. Pavlov's experiments which were typically, though not exclusively, based on elicited responses have since been treated as a sub-class of conditioning and tagged *classical*, an epithet that in the usage of psychologists carries no more respect than they will accord to the 'old style', whatever that be. Operant conditioning is also known as *instrumental*, stressing the instrumentality of the response. A connexion between it and the stimulus becomes established only if the latter has the reinforcing property of a pleasurable experience or of averting a disagreeable situation. Of course, in this paradigm neither S nor R corresponds to the meaning otherwise attributed to the term, and is used only to satisfy the conventions of behaviourist learning theory, even at the cost of logical clarity.

There are various techniques used for the instrumental conditioning of animals, pressing a bar in order to obtain food or to stop an electric shock being the most widely used. The method is flexible enough to make the response instrumental only if certain conditions are satisfied, for example, if a particular light is on or off, or if a certain interval has elapsed since the last reinforcing event. Animals can learn these cues but their discovery of them involves processes that are not strictly within the realm of learning as this term is defined in psychology.

In experiments with human subjects the mastery of these non-learning components of the task are even more important for successful performance, so that instrumental conditioning becomes a test of perceptual discrimination or problem solving rather than a simplified example of learning. Following the model of instrumental conditioning, a defect in human learning would be attributable to defects in perception or concept formation or memory, or other information processing operations, unless it were unequivocally traceable to some faulty association between emitted response and reinforcing stimulus. The spinster who made her first conquest in spite of a haughty and insulting manner may have developed this into a trait or style and have failed to find a suitor because of a severe flaw in instrumental conditioning.

Motor learning; rule learning

If conditioning paradigms serve as examples for the acquisition of neurotic personalites, for self-defeating rather than effective habits, it is because conditioning is a model *par excellenc*e of blind learning. There are, of course, also instances of effective behaviour that we learn blindly; the simple motor skills like walking are examples in point. Typically, though, even those skills are learnt by a process of trial and error and by a deliberate choice and modification of the instrumental response. Moreover, even at the level of motor behaviour, one does not learn a particular response by the use of a repertoire from which to choose that which best fits a situation and an action plan. Children do not learn all over the motions of running down stairs with each rise and depth of the tread; they learn a skill that is adjustable to the varied demands of different sized stairs, including the use of their bottoms if the gradient is too steep for their legs.

Conditioning and other associative theories of learning tell us little, if anything, about the manner in which the child learns to discriminate treads without actually incurring the penalty of a bruised knee or bleeding nose for taking the wrong step, or of the process by which stairs of diverse shapes, sizes and surfaces are brought under a common rule of locomotion. Experience with various types is necessary, but a few examples will suffice for quite successful generalization to many more instances than have ever been encountered before. The skill of descending a spacious well of winding marble steps can be transferred quite readily to a narrow and straight wooden staircase. Similarly, the player learns how to co-ordinate and sequence his movements so as to achieve a tactical goal, how to hit the ball hard at an exposed spot wherever that be in the field or court.

Learning, in the sense of practice and monitoring feedback information, seems necessary only for the acquisition of the basic motor skill which can then be applied with remarkable effectiveness in a wide variety of conditions – determined by the distribution of the field, by the direction and speed of the wind, etc. – none of which has previously been encountered in exactly the same combination. In command of the rules that relate to throwing or hitting angle and velocity, the player can solve an infinite number of boundary-value problems.

This observation on motor skills can be generalized to other types of learning. In regard to verbal learning, it is quite evident that children learn rules, else they would never say 'swimmed' or 'runned'. G. A. Miller (Miller, Galanter and Pribram, 1960) stated the case definitively when he estimated the number of grammatically correct and meaningful sentences a person utters in a lifetime, and the years he would require to learn each with only a single exposure and subsequent reinforcement. The proverbial threescore and ten would be quite insufficient to master even a child's simple chatter by the incremental method of learning theories. The solution to the puzzle posed by the vast number of grammatically correct and usually also meaningful sentences most of us are able to formulate is that we learn rules about the construction of sentences in a language. These rules enable us to 'generate' an infinite population of formally correct sentences and to reject with confidence sentences that are incorrect by the same standards. The rules, moreover, are remarkably elastic, as any one would be forced to admit after listening to a tape recording of a live discussion.

Disorders of learning thus may, but need not, stem from defective associations, whether these involve stimulus substitution or response substitution. They can be attributed to direct, and more typically to cumulative, failures in discrimination and categorization or to defects in the formulation and application of rules and plans. Some disorders may indeed stem from attempts to apply associative learning beyond its limits of effectiveness. One can learn a fair amount of history by the associative method, but only with the help of appropriate rules of categorization and transformation will one gain a firm grasp of the past. In mathematics the associative technique helps in learning the multiplication table but not much progress will be made without the mastery of a hierarchy of rules. The child who uses only associative learning methods – if there be such a one – may pass an elementary quiz but has as little hope of learning history as of learning mathematics.

Registration of Information

Perception and registration

Our environment consists of innumerable objects and events that are capable of making impressions by means of our sense organs. In fact, we perceive only a tiny fraction of that potential input and perceive most of it in some organized pattern. A circular design of thirty-six dots is seen as a circle, and a rectangular design of the same ingredients is seen as a rectangle. If required, we can see either design as a collection of thirty-six dots and we can even see the area within the dotted lines or the spaces between the dots, but we must be specially set to see them. Perception is selective and constructive; we perceive chiefly that which we expect to find in the environment, or that which conflicts with our expectations – figures and sounds that strike us because of their unfamiliarity or intensity or strategic position. As a rule we notice that which is significant to us – for our survival, for our lesser goals, for our values. Quite often we also misperceive objects and events in obedience to the same principles.

Now, just as we do not perceive all that is perceptible, we do not remember all that we perceive. We do not even remember those perceptual experiences that have quite decisively contributed to our learning, for example, the Chinese landscapes that have taught us to see perspective according to the oriental convention. Sudden disruptions in the flow of road traffic may be occasions for perfecting our driving skill, that is for learning, and such disruptions must be perceived if we wish to escape without damage or injury, but only rarely will they be remembered as specific occurrences. We listen to the patter of the rain or observe the blue sky through the window, and make very practical decisions about our clothes accordingly, but only exceptionally do we remember those decision processes or their outcome or the perceptual cues that were weighed in their course. Given either the decision or the cue, however, we could reconstruct the other with fair assurance.

Not everything that is perceived becomes part of our memory, not even all those percepts that have exerted an enduring effect on our behaviour. Must all memories have been perceived? The answer to this question is more difficult than would appear on first blush. The problem is not only that posed by conceptual memories, by examples of posthypnotic suggestion, by subliminal advertising and by unconscious impressions. Most of us have had some false memories, recollections of events that did not take place or at any rate happened quite differently from their reconstructed image. In fact all memories differ to some extent from the immediate percept of an event, whether that be heavily biased itself or reasonably veridical.

Elaboration of percepts

Memories are edited versions of immediate experience, edited according to certain well-documented laws. These comprise, first of all, simplification, abridgement, stress on salient features, omission of unimportant details and also the revision, modification and distortion of the content in conformity with certain values, intentions, generic types, etc. The memory of a first ball or stage appearance is notoriously embellished in recollection, but observations invested with far less personal significance are subject to the same forces of screening and moulding. As indicated in the previous chapter, the fallibility of memory unmitigated by doubt is familiar from the court room and has been demonstrated in the laboratory by experiments on testimony and on the spread of rumour.

An entertaining raconteur is admired for the skill with which he resurrects episodes that sound pretty dull if reported with painstaking accuracy. The confidence trickster who exercises the same skill for the sake of more crudely selfish interests, however, is mistrusted, or ought to be. One could draw a sharp line between the two types on the assumption that the first would be factual and strictly truthful if that were the conduct proper to the situation, while the latter could not even if he tried. The dividing line may not always be quite so distinct and there are many examples of semi-fictitious reports by perfectly ordinary people that serve no special goal – altruistic or selfish – and deviate from the factual beyond all power of recovery by the narrator. Examples are too trivial to cite and pose no serious problem except for the dilemma about the relationship of perception to memory.

There is quite enough evidence to show that most of the elaboration crept in after the stage of perception, possibly at some phase of retention, although more probably in the process of recall. The deluded patient who claims to have won the battle of Rivoli clearly remembers something he never perceived and we dismiss his claim as not a memory at all. Our verdict may be more hesitant in the face of a girl who reports having heard the voices of supernatural beings; she seems to have quite genuine memories although it is difficult to decide what she had actually perceived. You will be even harder put to classify the recollection of an acquaintance who vividly recalls meeting you at a conference in Sweden, when you equally vividly remember meeting him elsewhere and are sure that you

never attended a conference in Sweden. Each of you has
perceived the other on some previous occasion and seems
to remember that occasion but they are different occasions. Can only one of those recollections be based on
perception?

The acquisition of memories

Memories are typically based on perception more or less
closely, but not all the things perceived are remembered.
There is evidently a process that transforms percepts into
memories, that registers the incoming information so that
it can be recognized or recalled in some manner of likeness to the original. This process has been quite properly
called registration, although not every psychologist is
prepared to use the term, but then not every psychologist
believes that such a process is necessary to account for the
establishment of memories. Its recognition implies a distinction between the cumulative process of learning skills
or acquiring habits and of fixating impressions or filing
information for subsequent access. This distinction does
not overlap completely with those between blind and in-
sightful learning or between incremental and single-trial
learning. A child can register the experience of flying over
the Atlantic Ocean without understanding any of the
geographic or engineering accomplishments involved.
There are also many items of information, the names of
persons or of chemicals for example, that are registered
only after repeated presentation. It could be argued that
some incremental or latent learning preceded these instances of registration, but the fact of the matter is that,
given the need or interest, a single exposure is quite sufficient for learning such a name.

A process of registration is necessary to account for
certain disorders of memory and learning, when perception as tested by a matching task for example is faultless,
yet the same figure cannot be recognized after only a few
seconds and with no intervening event. These defects are
often treated as failures of memory – of short-term

memory – but such a classification does not distinguish between the operations of acquiring memories, putting information into storage, and those operations by which memories are recovered, taken from storage. Both experientially and behaviourally these are different operations and, theoretically at any rate, could be impaired independently of one another.

Rehearsal

Moreover, information available for immediate recall is not necessarily registered in a memory system. Information that has been quite clearly perceived and is well within the span of apprehension is likely to be lost within a few seconds unless some operations are performed to fixate it, to transfer it, according to Waugh and Norman's (1965) model, from a primary to a secondary memory store. The extremely rapid rate at which brief messages are lost beyond recovery has been demonstrated by Peterson and Peterson (1959) and by other experimenters using their technique. This consists of presenting consonant trigrams, for example VJT, for recall after delays ranging in length from three to eighteen seconds. The trigrams are usually presented vocally and each is followed immediately by a three-digit number. The subject's instruction is to proceed subtracting serial threes from the number, starting immediately on its presentation, e.g., 475; 472; 469. ... This he does until stopped by the instruction to repeat the last trigram, that is continuously over periods of three, six, ... eighteen seconds, and the purpose of this arithmetic exercise is to prevent him from rehearsing the trigram subvocally or aloud. Under these conditions a delay of nine seconds is enough to cut successful recall to one half of the trials and the proportion drops further still with longer retention periods.

Figure 1 presents the results of an experiment I conducted with healthy and intelligent young people, following the Petersons' design, but using single consonants, and combinations of two, four and five, as well as of three consonants for the message to be retained. This, like several other related experiments, points out the important part that repeating the message plays in verbal learning, and also raises some questions about the acquisition of information through other sensory channels. Covert re-

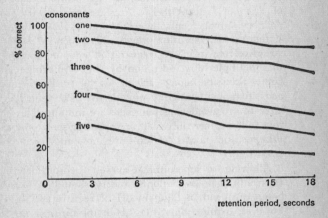

Figure 1 Retention of consonants with intervening counting

hearsal in the kinesthetic and proprioceptive modalities seems feasible, but hardly in vision, touch, or olfaction, nor does all the information monitored by these senses lend itself to verbal coding.

The finding that the retention curve drops steeply over a span of eighteen seconds in the Peterson-type experiment suggests that rehearsal prevents a rapid decay, whether that be a spontaneous process or the result of interference. Its effectiveness may be due to the opportunity rehearsal provides for the coding and organizing of messages, for the selection and formation of mediators, for transferring the information from a perceptual to a memory system. These seem to be the operations for the sake of which we would repeat aloud a name we wish to remember. Repetition without such intent should be of little value in learning and there is experimental evidence in support of this view.

Filing, categorization and mediators

The manner by which registration is achieved in the brain is known no better than are the neural mechanisms of learning skills. Other defects associated with severe memory derangements suggest that it is an operation of setting up and executing programme sequences. As reconstructed from its effects, registration seems to correspond to a multiple filing operation by which information becomes accessible along each of several tracks. Temporal and situational contiguity provide the most general principle of cross-indexing but there are innumerable others that follow either universally accepted or sometimes quite idiosyncratic norms of co-ordination and hierarchical trees.

Allowing for superordinate as well as co-ordinate links, the traditional associationist theory should be perfectly compatible with a filing model of registration. It does, however, require some rules about the direction associations will follow in a given situation, and must also allow for mediating processes. It was pointed out above that, at the level of conditioning, the range of new associations is limited by certain innate constraints. Similarly, it has been proposed, for example by C. G. Jung (1953), that some symbols, associations at the level of perception and abstract thought, are also archetypal, (that is, innate). They certainly can be learned, so that the ideas and emotions elicited by the sight of a heraldic eagle are entirely different from those evoked by a live bird on a rock and different in armies that rally around poles tipped with this emblem from armies that follow poles tipped with a horse-tail or banners decorated with a dragon.

The tendency to categorize the incoming data according to pre-established and universal or *ad hoc* subjective principles, as well as the part played by mediators, has been demonstrated in a variety of learning experiments; the latter especially with the paired-associate technique. A standard procedure is to use three lists of words, A, B and C, and start by presenting items from A paired with those from B, then, after a criterion of learning has been reached, present items from B paired with those from C, and finally A paired with C, always in the same order. Whether the learner recognizes the associative link provided by B between A and C or remains unaware of it, it is effective in facilitating the third learning task. Mediators need not be chosen and provided by the experimenter; subjects tend to find them spontaneously, although they may not always select the most effective mediators and indeed may fail to resort to this aid altogether.

A verbal medium may be the safest for the durable storage of much information, yet the initial associations necessary for learning could be established more effectively by means of, for example, pictorial mediators. Nevertheless adults and, as experiments have shown, older persons in particular are far more apt to choose a verbal mediator and often in accordance with a rigorous grammatical rule which, whatever its virtue, could demand more time to fit than is available. A flexibility in choosing the most appropriate mediators, as well as their availability may thus prove to be an important asset in many learning situations, an asset which if inadequate could indeed account for disorders in learning. The acquisition of a varied array of mediators and of a skill in their use undoubtedly makes a principal contribution to the process of learning to learn. People differ considerably in their propensity to apply this skill. Older persons, as Hulicka (Hulicka and Grossman, 1967) has shown in paired-associate experiments, are less apt to resort to mediators spontaneously than are young adults, although they are familiar with their use, for they benefit more from the instruction to find their own mediators.

Just as an image or a mnemonic trick can serve as a mediator for associating messages at the same level, pre-established patterns and devices help their hierarchical ordering in registration. Poetry is enriched by the unconventional application of mediators in imagery and causal construction; the utterances and thoughts typical of psychotic patients also reveal the operation of idiosyncratic mediators but these usually fail to serve the purpose of inter-personal communication. The creative artist strays deliberately from the well-worn associative tracks and must judge the boundaries up to which he will be followed. His special skill is in making correct judgements as well as in exploring new paths but he, too, may start on one and turn back with curiosity unsated. Here is an example from *Maiden Voyage* by Denton Welch (1943), the sensitive autobiographer who in retrospect discovered significance and beauty in so many seemingly trite childhood incidents: 'I poured a whole tin of mustard into my bath. It made the water look yellow and sticky and it stung a scratch on my finger, but I enjoyed it because it reminded me, for some reason, of the *Ingoldsby Legends*' (Penguin edn, p. 100). This is the moment for the leap into bisociation, as Koestler (1964) would have it, or for the recombination of previously established mediating processes in Hebb's (1949) terminology; but nothing follows, not even a laborious advance into association. There could be a flaw in the index rather than a failure in finding a rare cross reference.

Usually the thread that ties together personal experiences or items of information in memory is quite easily disentangled from threads that tie the same recollections with yet others. Repeated events registered under a common generic heading are distinguished from all other members of that class by their unique contextual setting. We may just manage to remember most, perhaps even all, of the occasions we have been to the theatre but hardly ever visits to the bank. We do so, not because one of these experiences is more enjoyable or necessarily less frequent than the other, but because each play and performance differs from all others in more respects than the virtually ritual act of filling in a slip of paper and exchanging it for some cash. If one's call at the bank happens to coincide with the chance encounter of a friend one has not seen for many years, the occasion will stand out quite distinctly amidst all others. It will be tagged by the occurrence of something unexpected.

Anticipated significance

Events that conform to anticipation in every detail are not the substance of which memories are made. Unlike the drive forced into many detours by processions on the main thoroughfares, that which progresses smoothly from home to work will not provide material for three minutes' worth of conversation on our arrival. Experiences are remembered the better the more information they contain in the sense of their unpredictability. Indeed, an event must be unpredictable in some degree in order to qualify as an event, as something distinct from all the happenings that surround it. Registering it is a process of matching the incoming information against some model and the expectancy will also determine to some extent the manner in which it will be filed for future reference.

One of the filing instructions concerns the anticipated relevance of the information. It cannot be accidental that we usually remember our room number while we are staying in a hotel but forget it as soon as we move on; that we can reconstruct the cards played in a game of bridge as long as that information helps our play; that we hold the instructions where to turn left and right in a station while we are passing through it and then rapidly disencumber ourselves of this map unless we expect to be back again and attempt to fixate it. Most readers of fiction can recall the names of characters for just as long as they are necessary to follow the plot and then shed that information or allow it to fuse into some composite image with similar residual features from other novels. Repetition is only one determinant of learning and retaining such information. If the game of bridge was an unusually difficult one, the station an important place in our life, if the book contains a story we look forward to discussing with another reader, a single exposure may suffice to make a lasting impression, to last for as long as it has some significance.

Our estimates of future utility may be in error on occasions but those are the exceptions. The manner by which we arrive at them varies. Sometimes it is a deliberate decision but more often it is done automatically by means of some unconscious calculation that takes into account the probabilities of relevant future events on the basis of the past occurrence of similar situations. Interest, of course, has a lot to do with it. An opera fan who can list the cast of five hundred performances may not be able to recite a single cricket eleven he has watched in the field and may not even bother to read their names on the score card. He can perceive the difference between the tall and heavy fast bowler and the sparsely built spinner but the difference is not significant enough to register in memory, for he does not expect that at any future date he will want to revive an image of or talk about the match.

Nobody knows what the limits are, if there be such limits, of the amount of information the human mind can store. It is, however, quite probable that beyond certain limits the more data are filed the longer it takes to find those that are wanted and also the greater the chance of misfiling or of returning with an incorrect message. There are undoubtedly economic reasons for discarding some information altogether and for placing some in the rear files. These operations are performed quite effectively and in a remarkably orderly manner if judged on criteria of biological usefulness, personal value and interest, and other relevant considerations. Clearly, the process of registration also includes some decisions about the term for which some item of information is to be held, in other words an instruction about forgetting it.

Efficient learners should also be efficient forgetters. Underwood (1957) has reported some experimental evidence in support of this law. His trained learners did much better than naïve subjects in a test of immediate recall of nonsense syllables but twenty-four hours later remembered considerably less of the material. Many a student can confirm the same law from his personal experience of memorizing passages the night before an examination. If he succeeds thanks to special learning skills applied to the task, one component of those skills is the ability to acquire information for a limited retention period.

Coding and transformation

Registration thus entails selection, cross filing, disposition about length and access of storage; all processes carried out in the brain with enduring effects on its structure and function. Registration also involves operations of transformation and coding, since visual images cannot be stored exactly as they form on the retina, and information received through the other sensory channels is even less suitable for isomorphic recording. Much of the information we register is not perceptual at all. Concepts, abstractions, relationships, rules and plans can only be recorded and stored in codes. Even visual maps that would seem perfectly suited for topographical recording are more efficiently registered in codes. Chess players report that in their mental flow charts the men on the board are represented by the vectors of their moves: the castle not as a crenellated bastion but as a Greek cross.

Coding may involve grouping the data, condensation and other tactics of ordering, but typically also entails information reduction. The transformations by which information is reduced in registration vary in difficulty. Memorizing the image of a bull depicted on the wall of the Lascaux caves should be easier than memorizing Piero della Francesca's mural narrative of the Legend of the Cross because prehistoric art demanded a greater degree of information reduction than the Renaissance. The Renaissance painters, in turn, reduced the information found in

sacred and mythological texts. The information reduction
and coding operations are quite obvious in narrative
painting but are equally present in landscapes and still
lives, both in the creative process and, as Gombrich (1960)
has demonstrated, in the spectator's mind, although his
transformation is more likely to result in the enhancement
of information.

Thanks to information theory the magnitude of the
transformation involved in coding can be determined
quantitatively and this is what Posner and Rossman
(1965) did in an experiment of short-term retention
which, among other things, also demonstrated that lapse
of time is not necessarily a major determinant of forgetting. They divided their subjects into four groups and
presented them with strings consisting of four pairs of
randomly chosen digits. Each group had a different instruction: (a) to repeat the pairs in reverse order; (b) to
add them up; (c) to group them according to a fourfold
classification into high-odd, high-even, low-odd and low-
even; and (d) to lump together high-odd and low-even as
against low-odd and high-even.

The four tasks involved information reduction by 0,
2·8, 4·6, and 5·6 bits, that is binary units of information
transmitted. Although the subjects were asked to repeat
the entire string, their performance was scored only with
regard to the first pair which itself was always exempted
from the transformation. Retention varied with the difficulty of the transform, being highest following reversal
of the order. Whether immediate recall under these conditions tests short-term memory or registration, it is evident
that some information is apt to be lost in the process of
its coding for retention and, as shown by another experiment of the same investigators, the loss depends more on
the difficulty of the transform than on the number of
intervening and therefore potentially interfering items
listed, or on the length of delay before recall.

Still another experiment of these investigators shows
the enhancing effect of transformation on the retention of

a message. Transformation, of course, demands some attention and that would increase the probability of re-membering the information that undergoes the process. Up to a point the greater complexity of the transforma-tion may increase the chances of correct recall but it is also likely to increase the incidence of errors and of those alterations that are necessary to fit some information into a pre-existing schema. Defects in learning and in memory could arise from this process and would differ according to the learner's capacity to perform the required trans-formations, as well as his access to appropriate coding templates.

3 Remembering and Forgetting

Retention

You can think of retention in the sense of a vessel or a living organism holding a fluid, or alternately in the sense of a growing tree retaining its shape. In regard to learning and memory the first metaphor is misleading, since neither the behavioural nor the neural scientist can point his finger to anything that could be kept intact or could leak through a crack. Very likely there are changes in the brain tissue whenever something is learned or memorized, and such changes are lasting in their effects yet susceptible to erosion, but no one knows where to find them. The behavioural scientist infers retention from its observable effects, somewhat like the shape of the tree from its silhouette against the sky. He thinks of retention as a condition that intervenes between registration or acquisition and recall or recognition, though hardly as a continuous process in the sense in which he must account for these performances.

The acquisition of a skill or of some information is a finite event, although it may be accomplished incrementally on successive occasions. It can be accomplished only by means of some continuous process in the central nervous system and can be interrupted both by direct intervention, such as an electric shock, or by an indirect disturbance, such as a distracting or competing activity. The same is true of the process of remembering, whether that consists of the exercise of a learned skill or the retrieval of some message. Retention, however, cannot be a continuous neural process, for it persists through disruptions of central nervous system activity and through distractions of all kinds and severity. Learning or information placed in permanent storage is impervious to electric or mechanical shock, to freezing or drugs, to the emotional stresses and cognitive loads of life experiences, but can undergo lawful changes with these experiences.

Schemata

With habits, skills and other accomplishments, the process of schematization is quite evident. Enthusiasts of children's 'art' deplore the instruction given in perspective, in techniques of observation and reproduction, for once a child has learned to draw things as they appear to him, he will no longer be able to draw as he thinks about them, the way he used to draw. Having mastered the skill of riding a bicycle, he cannot reproduce the exercises by which he attained that accomplishment – except under hypnosis perhaps. So it is also with some memories that resemble more closely the latest recollection than the original event or become a composite of several successive experiences with a common principle theme. Learning progresses by degrees toward mastery, memories undergo modifications. All this indicates the operation of some ongoing process in the brain. That retention involves some such continuous activity has been widely assumed and most notably by the Gestalt psychologists who view memory traces as acting in constant communication with each other, and who emphasize the trend in these traces over time towards better, simpler forms. While the Gestalt psychologists were concerned chiefly with visual figures, Stern (1938) analysed the organization tendencies in verbal material and found that reduction to logical terms, prejudices, interpretations and additions altered the content without the narrator's awareness of deviating from the original.

A record that is subject to continual and progressive modification as a result of its interaction with other records hardly fits one's image of a trace. Some learning, certain types of memory may indeed be firm in outline and structure, immutable in content, static as well as stable. Other types are flexible, programmatic, subject to frequent or continual modification. Remembering uses schemata as well as traces. Bartlett introduced this concept into the psychology of remembering, deriving it from Head, the neurologist, who had used schema in reference to man's postural model of himself which, although it changes all the time, yet serves as a standard for subsequent postural changes. Bartlett (1932) took from Head (1920) the principle of an active organization of successive impressions, or their corresponding responses by which experiences of the past systematically influence those of the present. This active organization is the schema to which successive experiences contribute in a cumulative order rather than as distinct traces.

This dynamic model of the memory schema distinguishes it from another concept which also involves information reduction, that is, the generic type, the assembly of a few defining attributes such as caricaturists use to depict their stock characters and, less conspicuously, everybody relies on when drawing, for example, a fish, a seascape or a family gathering. Bartlett's concept of the schema is like the chess player's map which is constantly brought up-to-date and seen – particularly in blindfold play – as a pattern of positions and moves rather than of pieces. Recalling the state of the game at any specific earlier stage can be achieved only by some reconstructive effort.

Serial reproduction

In a group of experiments of serial and repeated reproduction – the one using several subjects in a chain like the telephone game, the other using successive attempts by the same subject – Bartlett illustrated his thesis that remembering is a reconstructive effort after meaning, that impressions are not recorded photographically but in a pattern to fit a pre-established schema. The reconstructive process in remembering is most clearly apparent when the original image or message is unfamiliar, ambiguous or fragmentary. The cursorily articulated hieroglyph of an owl, the *mulak* of ancient Egypt, satisfies all these requirements and in ten stages of serial copying it underwent the progressive transformation shown in Figure 2; waning and waxing in size, the wing turning into a tail, the ears sharpening, until it assumed the perfectly distinct portrait of a kitten from the rear, with a bow around its neck.

Figure 2 Progressive transformations of an Egyptian mulak *into a portrait of a kitten during serial reproduction. (Reproduced from F. C. Bartlett (1932), Remembering, Cambridge University Press, p. 180, with permission of the publisher)*

With any but the simplest designs we take it for granted that reproductions from memory will not produce exact replicas of the model. With verbal material it is commonly assumed that recall, if not strictly verbatim, should at the most deviate from the original by substituting synonyms, omitting frills and perhaps condensing some phrases. This may be a legitimate assumption with some kinds of material but not with descriptive texts. Using several rather sketchy and partly obscure prose passages, for example an Indian folk tale, as well as reports of sports matches and scientific debates, Bartlett demonstrated the formative influence of personal interests, attitudes and emotional involvements on the products of recall. The contractions, alterations in content and enrichment with imported material that these stories underwent in serial reproduction revealed some quite systematic and identifiable trends. Both content and style changed progressively from the exotic or individual to the conventional. There was a tendency toward the concrete, yet proper names and definite numbers would be omitted or varied. The texts were radically abbreviated, except where elaborations were needed to resolve ambiguities. Opinions, conclusions, epithets were apt to be reversed, incidents transposed, details selected for emphasis, at times in obvious accordance with the subject's personal preoccupations and values or cultural norms.

Bartlett's most widely quoted example was a story notable for its gaps, ambiguities and unfamiliar content. I. H. Paul (1959) proceeded to examine the influence of these attributes on the distortions and fragmentations that stories undergo in serial recall. He found that familiarity offered no protection from a sizable loss of content but that it preserved the coherent structure of a narrative, while gaps were likely to cause degradation on both these counts. Where gaps created ambiguities, extraneous material would be brought in for explication and it was the type of person otherwise least given to importation who was likely to use the borrowed content for interpretation; the opposite type tended to use it for mere decoration or sharpening. In serial recall only explicatory importations influenced subsequent reproductions. The function of explication is to promote both familiarity and coherence, the principal attributes of a schema that facilitate new learning as well as remembering.

Apart from its occasional service as a parlour game, serial reproduction is not a very common technique for the transmission and conservation of messages. Its use in psychological research is justified on the ground that it allows for the simulation, within a relatively short time span, of changes that take place in normal remembering over much longer terms. In a research I conducted on the amnesic syndrome this technique also enabled me to repli-cate in perfectly healthy persons some of the anomalies that characterize the reproductions of amnesic patients in immediate recall. One of the texts in my experiment was the following news report culled from a morning paper :

In a city in India, several thousand schoolchildren paraded in the main square to celebrate the sixty-eighth brithday of the Prime Minister. While reviewing the parade the Prime Minister released a number of doves, the symbols of peace, from the cages in which they had been kept. The white doves flew over the heads of the young marchers. One of them, however, perched atop the Prime Minister's head while he took the salute.

The patients reported in immediate recall rather less than one quarter of the sixteen content units into which this story was divided, but transformed other units and gratuitously added information that seemed to fit. The tendency to be more exact or more conclusive than seems desirable for news reporters was particularly marked in attempts to give the number of the children on parade or of the doves released and in rounding out the story with such observations as 'the children were watching the dove until it flew away' or 'they were cheering. The Prime Minister thought they were cheering him; they were actually cheering the dove.'

Under similar circumstances normally functioning people would stick closer to the original but in serial reproduction, at the end of a short chain of three, in which each link reproduced the text presented to him after a delay of twenty-four hours, the final product turned out to be remarkably similar to the immediate reproduction of the amnesic patients. In contrast to Bartlett's finding, definite numerical estimates appeared gratuitously as they did in the patient's reports – 64 white doves, 2000 pigeons, 30,000 school children. The subjects of this experiment also resorted to interpretations of the occasion and to comments on how amusing the scene must have looked in order to complete the story, as did the amnesic patients. I could hardly anticipate as close a parallel as I discovered between the following ending of a patient's immediate report: 'Prime Minister had sixty-eight doves to celebrate his birthday. When he went to count the doves, one was missing, as it was perched on his head', and this conclusion of the final reproduction in serial recall: 'In honour of this occasion he released a flock of doves; 44 in number; 43 turned up, the 44th he couldn't find, for it was perched on his head.'

There is another virtue in using the test of serial or repeated reproduction. The procedure involves discrete attempts at recall on successive occasions. The changes the text or image undergoes – contraction, simplification, emphasis, assimilation to some pattern or norm, enrichment – are cumulative in their effect; they progress stepwise along recognizable courses. We can watch in slow motion the continuous process that is otherwise observable only in its end result. Furthermore, we observe these changes in retention as they occur in discrete trials of recall, in situations that are quite unequivocally attempts to meet a demand of the situation, for which the information retrieval systems of the brain must be activated.

The changes that memories seem to undergo in retention could in fact occur in the process of recall. If a single attempt at recall should appear to be too sudden an occasion to accommodate the substantial modifications that are observed over widely spaced trials in repeated or serial reproduction, then the effect could be attributed to successive subvocal revivals of the record. Such an argument would get around the difficulty posed by the assumption that retention is a continuous ongoing process, but in fact rests on an equally gratuitous assumption, for there is no evidence whatever that information is in fact held over long periods by means of periodic unobservable rehearsals. It is, however, quite probable that whenever some new information is registered on the memory files, the previous relevant records are reactivated to assimilate it and are modified in the process. Isolated memories should thus be the most resistant to change.

Trace model; decay

Speculations about the mechanism of retention are based largely on the trace model of memories which goes back to Plato who likened memory to the imprint of a seal on a block of wax. Wax being a substance liable to lose its shape, the image engraved on its surface is subject to spontaneous decay. The notion of spontaneously fading memory traces has a strong intuitive appeal, since most of our forgetting is gradual and seems to be unrelated to any other circumstances than the passage of time. Time, of course, can no more cause forgetting than it causes the corrosion of a girder, but the cerebral mechanism that subserves lasting memory could dissipate progressively with the passage of time. There is some evidence in the experimental literature to support the theory of spontaneously fading memory traces and much more that agrees with the view that forgetting is the result of some interference with the memory trace.

The trace model implicitly assumes that learning and memories are established and retained by a unitary process, whether incrementally or with a single impression. In so far as it allows for the coding operations in registration, they must precede the formation of the trace. Those filing operations, however, that provide for the future availability of the message must take place afterwards, since during the formation of the trace, the newly acquired information is very labile and vulnerable to decay. The trace gradually strengthens and then having reached an optimum stability by its contextual setting gradually weakens. Such a waxing and waning of the memory trace best fits a model of two or more successive retention processes which partly overlap and reach their peak at different times. This dynamic model, however, spoils the metaphor, since a sequence of functionally related but dissimilar biological processes cannot be properly likened to the formation of a discrete trace. In fact, trace has been used to refer to whatever changes in the brain may correspond to learning and to memories, that is to apparently several distinct biological processes.

Dual trace model

Hebb, for example, in his influential book *The Organization of Behavior* (1949), proposed a dual trace mechanism, according to which information is held for short periods by an ongoing neurophysiological action in the brain. By means of a neural after-discharge and a reverberatory cycle, a stimulus could be active for a while following its impact, but this effect is closely limited in duration and liable to spontaneous decay. The activity trace, however, promotes the formation of a more durable memory trace by facilitating a structural change in the brain. Structural memory traces are either impervious or, at any rate, are far less susceptible to spontaneous decay than activity traces. The dual trace model of memory has been subjected to criticism and rejected by some investigators on the ground that failures in short- and long-term memory can be accounted for by the same explanatory principles and more especially by provocative and retroactive interference, and that forgetting curves in short- and long-term memory look much the same.

Theirs is hardly a conclusive argument, since there are only a certain number of ways in which information can be forgotten or misremembered; moreover, identical manifestations could be traced to several different mechanisms. It seems more likely that a dualist model may not accommodate all the various mechanisms involved in the establishment and conservation of learning. This could be the conclusion drawn from an experiment in which Hebb (1961) presented his subjects with twenty-four nine-digit numbers for immediate recall. Each number contained every digit but zero in a different order, except that the third number occurred repeatedly in the sixth, ninth and every successive third position. Although the subjects were not advised about this feature of the experimental design and possibly did not notice it, their recall of that number progressively improved with each repeated trial and became far superior to their recall of the other nine-digit numbers.

Hebb concluded from this experiment that the immediate recall of a nine-digit number could not be subserved by an activity trace, since that would not endure long enough to account for the cumulative learning effect. Evidently, even a single hearing of the number resulted in the formation of some structural trace, although in all likelihood that was not the same kind of structural change in the brain that would correspond to a long-lasting memory. There have been other observations and experiments that argue for the assumption of several mechanisms, each subserving retention over different time spans and each operating in conjunction with the others. Hebb's intermediate trace may indeed correspond to the consolidation phase of memory.

Consolidation

Consolidation is a process inferred from the observation that under certain circumstances information received and quite adequately processed for the purpose of an immediate response can be completely erased from the memory files. Patients following electroconvulsive shock treatment, epileptic seizures and concussions of the brain have supplied extensive data on *retroactive amnesia*. They have no recollection whatever of the events that took place immediately prior to those disruptions of their normal brain function even though they played an intelligent, observant and active part in them. The extent of their retroactive amnesia varies considerably but is undoubtedly in excess of the life span of a reverberating neural discharge in the brain. There have been quite a few experiments with rats and other animals that have demonstrated the damaging effect of electric shock applied to the brain on new learning and similar effects have been produced by the application of chemical agents that depress brain activity.

Chemical treatment allows the experimenter to restrict learning to one of the hemispheres of the animal's brain and then investigate the conditions of transfer to the other hemisphere. Following this method Albert (1966a) observed that a single trial seemed sufficient for bilateralizing a unilaterally learned response but that following another application of potassium chloride to the originally untrained hemisphere this effect was lost. Learning by this artificial means of intracerebral transfer, like new learning with the entire brain, needs time for consolidation in order to last.

The time required for consolidation varies with species, with individual members of the species, with the content and complexity of the skill or information to be learned and remembered, with various situational conditions. It is not known what else is needed for the process of consolidation to be effective apart from time, except that certain central nervous system stimulants seem to enhance the process in mice, and at least one chemical agent that inhibits protein synthesis in the brain exerts the opposite effect. This agent puromycin radically alters the electroencephalographic pattern when injected into the brain, while cycloheximide does not, although it also inhibits cerebral protein synthesis. By the evidence of the experiments that demonstrated this effect, it seems that a protracted neuroelectric process in the hippocampus is necessary for the consolidation of new learning and that the activity can take as long as two days in mice. Structural damage in that area of the brain is known to impair the capacity for new learning.

There is thus at least one phase in retention that corresponds to a continuous activity of the brain, although it could be argued that consolidation belongs more to the process of registration than to retention. Either way, it represents a process additional to that performance in registration which is tested by immediate or very short-term recall. It may correspond to some operations of cross filing, of embedding the new information in the context of previous records, and involve additional recoding and other reorganizing manoeuvres. In the course of these some information will be lost and that which is preserved could be subjected to further modifications, similar to those that occur in serial reproduction. These transformations could indeed take place in several stages and continue over quite long stretches of time until the information is thoroughly schematized and then be resumed again as new data are grafted on or brought into the context of the schema. Speculation with so little solid foundation to build upon is hard to justify but, in this instance, it should serve the purpose of stressing that whatever retention may be it cannot be an inert state of storage.

Forgetting

Forgetting is inferred in exactly the same way as retention is and is also in danger of being taken for a static condition, especially if one uses a container or a wax tablet model of memory; the container is seen as drained, the grooves that were engraved on the wax tablet as smoothed over. Everyone has experienced occasions when some knack or piece of information was unavailable and later, perhaps when one felt less tired or preoccupied, it came back. Forgetting was not tantamount to losing something, it was rather an example of being unable to find it, a failure in those searching operations that are involved in remembering. When the wanted name is just out of reach, on the tip of one's tongue, the methodical search aspect of recall is quite apparent. One snatches at whatever clue is at hand; the first letter, the acoustic pattern of the missing word, and systematically explores the paths that may lead to it. Of course, the clues can be misleading and the search could fail for other reasons as well, but often enough it reaches its goal. With highly practised skills, with much rehearsed messages, there is no need to search and total forgetting rarely occurs, but the possibility of imperfect or partial recall is not negligible.

Because forgetting is so commonly a case of temporary failure rather than of a permanent incapacity, it has been argued that nothing a person learns or experiences is ever fully lost to him. This was a cardinal tenet of such diverse students of psychopathology as, for example, Bergson (1911), Freud (1960) and Bleuler (1924). A literal interpretation of this proposition appears unconvincing and quite incompatible with the argument that a good deal of information is registered with an explicit or implicit intent to jettison it after a while, or with the view that learning and memories tend to become schematized.

The beginner's crude skill is subsumed in the mastery of the accomplished performer; a sequence of closely similar experiences tends to blend into a generic memory without each retaining its identity. Hypnosis and free association techniques, however, have elicited recollections of precisely such discrete memories as would normally submerge in a schema. Freud accounted for their preservation by a dual registration theory of experiences – as memory images available in normal remembering and as sensory images that persist in their original form, free from subsequent accretions, but are available only in dreams, hallucinations or free association. The observations that called for this explanation are insufficient to confirm the theory and the basic proposition that no memory is ever completely lost is itself untestable. Freud (1961) modified it late in life

(1930), being content with the statement that nothing that was in the mind need ever perish. The principle of spontaneous decay certainly entails complete destruction, while the several mechanisms of interference are compatible both with an intact preservation of all learning and memories and with their partial dissipation.

Retroactive interference

If a memory, a learnt response, is not available once or on repeated occasions this can reasonably be attributed to the action of some prohibitory or rival agency which prevents its emergence. The source of the impediment may be an affect, a fear or aversion associated with the content of the memory or with the anticipated outcome of the response; it may be the interference of a prepotent rival memory or response that takes its place, gets confused with it or neutralizes it. To begin with psychologists assigned this meddlesome role primarily to learning that followed the acquisition of the unavailable response or memory and which was therefore viewed as exerting a retroactive interference. If you read two intricate novels with much the same plot and background in rapid succession, you are quite likely to transpose in recollection some characters and incidents from the second into the setting of the first. This is even more certain to happen if you learn two lists of nonsense words in close succession as has been demonstrated in countless laboratory experiments. The less articulated, the less codable some message, the sooner it is followed by a closely similar but different message, the more vulnerable it is to retroactive interference.

Interference between two successive learning experiences is not all unidirectional. Some details of the first novel may well displace incidents from the second and the earlier learned nonsense list is apt to interfere with the learning of that which follows it. For many decades proactive interference occupied a second place to retroactive as an explanation of forgetting until Underwood

(1957) lifted it into the front rank as a factor in verbal rote learning. Several experimenters have since demonstrated the adverse effect of previous learning on the verbatim recall of lists of unconnected words or of meaningful texts. In some instances, however, the effect of proactive interference could be shown only in the recall of the second or third item of a homogeneous series, and in every instance it is a residual effect manifest in diminishing the increment from proactive facilitation and practice. Understandably enough, one must exercise caution in generalizing from such a highly artificial and restricted laboratory observation to real life situations.

Proactive interference and facilitation

Proactive interference is thought to exert its effect as an earlier association, extinguished in the process of new learning, recovers in time. Basic to this theory is a general model of learning that consists of so many discrete and specific associations between stimuli and responses, a model that barely fits the facts of much human learning and remembering. Early learning, that is learning in early childhood, indeed must proceed by the establishment of innumerable entirely new associations but, as the child has built up a basic repertoire of skills and knowledge, his subsequent learning involves more and more transfer and new applications from that repertoire. Adult learning consists almost entirely of the recombination and subdivision of previously established associations and depends considerably on the judicious choice of a source of transfer for organizing, mediating, coding the novel information. Experiments in rote learning deliberately minimize the influence of positive transfer effects and thus allow scope for proactive interference, but thereby also narrowly limit their relevance to much of human learning.

Transfer of learning, the acquisition of new information or skills on the foundations of earlier ones, the development of schemata, are all examples of proactive facilitation, as are those practice effects that take place within a series of trials. Proactive interference may be a by-product, observed in recall, of proactive facilitation in learning. Underwood noted that in his experiment proactive interference accounted for a 50% loss of retention in twenty-four hours, but he did not consider the number of trials needed to reach criterion on the consecutive days. It is quite possible that the subjects familiar with the task learned much faster the second day and that the loss of information attributed to proactive interference in recall ought to be balanced against the gain in acquisition due to proactive facilitation. In remembering, proactive interference may thus reduce, and possibly even prevail over, the effects of proactive facilitation, but it has yet to be shown under what circumstances this is likely to happen and whether those effects originate from the process of registration or arise in the course of the searching and matching operations of recall.

Retroactive interference obviously cannot occur in the process of registration. It could take place in the course of retention, causing 'unlearning', or in recall. The trace of the more recently learned response or message is thought to compete in recall with the earlier one and, because of its comparative recency, to prevail over it. Some such displacement of earlier impressions by later ones is quite apparent in learning and in memories that are in a continuous process of development, of schematization. Your first recollection of your children whom you see day after day is as they look, talk and behave now, and you may find it quite difficult to reconstruct their image of five years ago without the aid of photographs and sound recordings. Zangwill (1950) reported with considerable admiration the feat of a Korsakoff patient who, when asked to draw a woman and then a bus, accurately reproduced the style and model current ten years earlier. He commented that people with an intact memory would hardly equal this achievement. The correction of the schema, its being brought up to date in the intact brain, could happen as each successive image, each successive message on the same theme, is being registered. If so, the effect takes place in the retention of the earlier memory, perhaps in its implicit and unobservable recall, and not when its overt recall is demanded and fails.

Response-interference

There is a source of interference, however, that takes place in the process of recall and indeed originates in that process. Very likely there are several such sources of interference and they are collectively known as response-interference. The most fully documented example of response-interference affects free or ordered recall of a list of unrelated items such as digits or nonsense syllables. Experiments have shown that the digit span thus measured underestimates the subject's capacity to transmit information, usually referred to as short-term memory. Alternative procedures, that require of him the reproduction of only one item from the list, indicate that his span is larger than estimated by a test of complete enumeration. These experiments in partial recall, of course, do not disclose to the subject which item he will be tested on until after the presentation of the entire list, so that in order to succeed, no matter what the required item will be, he must remember them all. Since in partial recall he succeeds with longer lists than in free or ordered recall it is evident that the number of items available to him was larger at the moment of his interrogation than in the course of recital, that he loses information in the process of recall.

The cause of his losing information could be a rapid decay of traces but it seems rather an interference of those items that the subject has recited, or written down, or pointed to, with the remaining items that are still to follow. All kinds of responses demanded by a task, not only those involved in recall or recognition, are liable to interfere with successful recall and experiments suggest that this effect can be particularly damaging when certain items have to be specially tagged and held in reserve while the others are being delivered. Most experimental demonstrations of response-interference have been in tests of very short term retention, but the effect is present in and quite familiar from long-term recall. We often set out to make a number of points in support of our case, then get sidetracked with the first or second point and fail to recapture the remaining ones.

Response-interference that prevents the recovery of such information as has been well established in long-term memory is a temporary impediment. The same source of interference with the rehearsal of a message in the phase of registration, however, is likely to result in its permanent loss. Retroactive interference could completely destroy the effect of learning, although it is more likely to obscure it, to reduce its signal property, in other words, to make it less accessible. Under conditions of less noise, with better cues, with more persistence or more efficient tactics in search, the same information would be available for recall. There are clearly several sources from which failures in recall could arise and the observable record of partial or complete forgetting rarely provides a clue for deciding whether it is caused by some sort of trace interference or by sluggish search. Many striking examples of memory derangement are clearly instances of ineffective operations in information retrieval.

Partial recall

Forgetting can be partial as well as complete. Experimenters who depend principally on lists of arbitrarily compiled units or paired associates allow their subjects only the alternatives of success or failure. Performance scored for the number of units recalled or considerations of inversions in order, however, make allowances for partial recall, that is, for partial forgetting. Outside the laboratory there are also other ways in which skills or information learned can be partially forgotten and indeed this happens in all remembering that consists in the reconstruction from retained components. There are also

experimental demonstrations of partial remembering, for
example in procedures that provide prompting cues, such
as the first letters of words, and in recognition experiments that allow a second choice if the first was incorrect.
The number of correct second choices far exceeds the
chance probability based on random guessing. Outside
the laboratory everybody has had the experience of recalling a name, a number or of reproducing a manual
response only after repeated stabs at it, none of which
was quite right but possibly each came a little closer to
the required model than the preceding trial.

Recall

Registration, learning and retention are all inferred from
some performance; the recitation of a message, the exercise of a skill, some response that the organism did not
display previously in similar situations, especially if it
involves a more economical technique for mastering the
problem on hand. For those concerned with normal
remembering as well as with its disorders, of all these
performances, verbal recall of some information is by far
the most interesting. Recall involves the recollection of
some past personal experience or some previously registered information, vocally or in some recorded medium or
indeed in thought without any concomitant overt act.
Such a performance can be deliberate, that is, in response
to some explicit question or other contextual stimulus, or
fortuitous when an implicit contextual cue is assumed to
operate. Recall can thus be relevant to the total situation,
although plainly irrelevant or incorrect in response to the
question or to the task at hand.

Recognition and recall

While typically verbal, recall can be visual or tactile, manifested by means of manual reproduction or reconstruction. Information registered through certain modalities,

for example olfaction or touch, can be remembered only by recognition. Recognition and recall are usually regarded as alternate processes of remembering, the first as less demanding than the latter. It is quite true that both normal people and patients with memory disorders often succeed in recognizing that which they cannot recall at will, or recognize a person as familiar when they cannot recall who he is or where they have met him. All such instances of recognition involve a measure of success in recall, that is of recalling an occasion, albeit a non-specific one, when one previously met the person.

Similarly, recall does not exclude recognition or even its discriminatory operations, for every process of recall terminates with some implicit act of recognition. The person who remembers recognizes his memory as correct, as fitting the demands of the situation and does so alike whether his judgement of a match is objectively correct or false. His judgement of a match must emerge in the process of remembering, for there is no homunculus inside his head who knows in advance what it is that constitutes the proper memory. The mechanism of recognition is completely unknown and has at best been described metaphorically as, for example, by John Lehmann (1954) who, with reference to Proust, compares memory to a 'sentry waiting for a password that one cannot possibly know beforehand.' Neural scientists who are hopeful of 'cracking the code' of memory storage are likely to come up against a tougher puzzle when they attempt to discover the mechanism by which the information selected from the store or the overt response is identified as appropriate. They have proposed various models of comparator mechanisms, typically based on a scanning operation, which indeed could serve the recognition of perfect identity. But the model must also provide for partial and imperfect identity, for the intuitive recognition of likeness in apparent diversity, for the bisociative process which Koestler (1964) regards as the gist of artistic creation, scientific discovery, and humour.

Even though recognition and recall may thus be inseparable processes, it is perfectly reasonable to treat the two as distinct in accordance with the explicit operations performed. Recognition is less liable to failure or error than recall because typically it offers fewer opportunities for failure or error. The number of faces anyone has the occasion to classify as familiar or unfamiliar is smaller than the ensemble of names that could fit either class of faces. In experiments, too, the choice of words or objects from which a subject selects those he has previously learned is narrower than the universe of such words or objects. In recall the subject must himself set the limits and he does so by initially scanning a much vaster ensemble than is practicable in any test of recognition. Success in recognition, moreover, is also helped by cues and is thus compatible with memories less articulate, with learning of lesser 'strength' than is necessary for successful recall.

Experiments employing pre-established finite ensembles for learning have shown that recognition is not necessarily superior to recall. On the other hand, Shepard (1967) noted that memory for such material as thematic pictures may be virtually boundless if tested by recognition of familiarity after a single previous exposure. Since the universe of such pictures is practically unlimited, success in recognition must be attributed primarily to the ease with which familiarity can be determined in the face of such distinctive material. The very features that invest each picture with its distinctiveness would make performance by accurate reproduction quite difficult, as would minimal differences between two or more pictures in recognition tests. Tests of recall often demand choices between several closely similar items or events – two words alike in sound or print or meaning, two or more episodes of much the same theme, repeated encounters with the same person or situation. Scanning the relevant files, sorting out the suitable entries before matching each for fit, are operations that can trip recall any number of times.

In recognition the last of these is the only one that needs
to be negotiated with certitude.

Immediate recall tests

One of the difficulties in recall is the control of all the
information that is involved in the task. The material may
exceed in content the limits of immediate grasp; it may
re-emerge in a scrambled order; it may evoke related
memories that are quite irrelevant to the task at hand and
crowd the registers with them. Effective recall must shut
out the noise, restore the original order, piece together the
units that can be handled at a time. That these operations
rapidly push the human brain to the limits of its capacity
is evident from experiments in immediate recall. Although
described as tests of short-term memory, these procedures
do not test memory in the sense of introducing some
delay or distraction between registration and recall. Rather
do they explore the limits of a subject's capacity to transmit series of unrelated message items, that is, his span of
apprehension or attention span.

The messages in experiments on immediate recall typically consist of digits or letters or words strung together
without any thread of meaningful connexion. They are
read aloud or shown in print to the subject at a steady
rate, fast or slow, one at a time and when the end of the
string has been reached he has to repeat as much of it as he
can. If the test is in ordered recall he must observe the
original sequence of the items; if it is in free recall all he
has to do is to reproduce the content in any order that
suits him. Under the latter conditions he is likely to start
off with the last few items and then follow up with some
that were further back in the list. The span of immediate
recall is quite limited; with digits ordered, reproduction
rarely exceeds or even reaches a run of nine, and four to
five is the average for normal young adults.

Patients with very severe memory disturbances usually
report about as many digits in this type of test as do
healthy people. For this reason alone, the standard digit

span is not a true test of memory. More suitable for that purpose is the running digit span in which the strings presented for recall predictably exceed the subject's retention capacity but he is not expected to recall them in full. In the standard digit span the subject is first tested on a short list and if he reproduces it without error he is next given a list that is longer by one item, and so forth until he reaches a level at which his performance fails. In the running digit span test he begins with strings above that range in length and is asked to reproduce the final items only, say the last five or as many from the end as he can, always in the original order. Of course, if he knew in advance the length of each string, he would try to ignore all of it that precedes the terminal segment and start to memorize the digits only as he reaches that point. In order to preclude such tactics, it is usual to test the running digit span with strings of randomly varying length.

Patients with memory defects perform poorly on this task, but that does not make performance in the running digit span a performance of memory, although it may justify its use to assess their capacity of learning and remembering. Recall in this task, as in the standard digit span, follows presentation with a minimal time lag, and all the intervening interference originates from the message itself. These conditions qualify the running digit span for a test of registration. It is quite apparent, though, that the running digit span involves operations that are also necessary for efficient delayed recall. Since the test strings exceed the span of immediate recall and the method of presentation tends to prevent rehearsal, the common feature of this test and of long-term recall is transmission of information under overload conditions.

Tests of the digit span or word span are so constructed as to preclude those coding tactics by means of which information is registered for future recall. Attempts to discourage normal human subjects from resorting to organizing principles are never fully successful, but the technique of these and like experiments in short-term re-

tention gets as close to that goal as any that employ verbal
material drawn from a language familiar to the subject.
One may, therefore, properly raise the question whether
performance in those tasks has any bearing on such problems as reconstructing from memory the farming methods
employed by a certain community or remembering where
to find some illuminating statistics on recidivism. The
common thread is the formidable amount of information
that, even when susceptible to efficient organizing strategies, has to be marshalled in these situations. Faced with
such a task, it may indeed matter but little whether the
information sought was first heard only a few seconds
earlier or must be pulled together from several more
distant occasions.

Reconstruction

Recall is a reconstructive process, even at the level of the
running digit span; it consists of the selection, ordering
and patterning of data, as well as of their retrieval from
storage. These two aspects of the performance are, of
course, interdependent; the creative process depends on
the availability of facts and themes and in turn draws in
additional data to fill gaps and round out designs. Associations are undoubtedly the mechanism by which material
is gathered in recall but the associations that will be operative on any one occasion are not all predetermined by what
happened in registration and possibly also in the course of
retention. They are very largely so determined in immediate recall and with rote learning, less so in delayed recall
and with material learnt for its meaning, and probably
least in retrospective recollections of life experiences and
past thoughts.

Total recall

Verbatim recall, the exact reproduction of a movement or
of an object, as has been proposed above, is a limiting case
and comparatively rare occurrence. There are indeed persons who have the capacity described as 'total recall'; they

have been reported but not adequately described or studied. Total recall is by no means an unmixed blessing, for it seems to be coupled with an inability to sort out, edit and efficiently inter-relate the material available. Whether this grave deficiency is a necessary concomitant of total recall is a matter yet to be determined by empirical investigation. Eidetic imagery, the ability to project on a blank screen a picture after its removal from view and to focus on any of its details has been reported to be quite common in children but rare in adults; it seems to be lost as the person acquires an analytic and abstractive method of information processing. He retains the ability to learn verbal material in rote fashion but does not often exercise it and may not choose to reproduce passages verbatim even though he could do so.

Level of abstraction

With information that is readily available, one has the option of recalling it at any of several levels of abstraction, and the choice must be conveyed by some sort of instruction to the mechanisms which transfer the data from a storage system into effector processes. Similarly, an instruction is needed regarding the rule by which the content of the memory or the response is to be reconstructed from the available data. Of course, this decision is itself a feat of memory, since one has to remember which rule is applicable in a given situation unless the situation provides the necessary cue. A request for a summary of the plot of *Antigone* precludes lengthy quotations in the original or in translation and contrariwise, the occasions are rare when a paraphrase would be acceptable for the *Salute to the Flag*. The limits of fidelity appropriate to a situation or task must, of course, be learned and remembered, and fitted to the closest available programmes for transformation. People who recall most texts more effectively by content than literally, nevertheless can recite certain messages only in rote fashion and must go back to the beginning if they get stuck halfway;

others can only learn by heart and may reproduce odd snatches of the original without filling in the gaps with their own words even though encouraged to do that.

Cues

Situational cues can determine the content as well as the manner of recall, inhibit as well as facilitate the process. A typical example of their facilitating effect is furnished by the novelist Nabokov (1966) who, in his autobiography, relates his first visit to Cambridge many years after his undergraduate studies there. His one-time tutor completely failed to recognize him until the visitor accidentally kicked over a tea tray that was placed on the floor, thus reproducing a gaffe he had committed the first time he had called on him. An example of the inhibitory effect of situational cues is provided by another incident from an academic setting. A colleague once told me how, while attending a convention and talking with a group of psychologists, a familiar person walked past and they exchanged greetings. Although my informant was sure that he knew that man quite well, he could neither recollect his name nor place him. A few days later, returning to his university, he met him again and immediately recognized him as the professor of archaeology. Travelling on personal business, this archeologist happened to pass through a convention of psychologists where he did not belong and where all logical cues led away from him.

Many people who had mastered a first language before acquiring another they have been using latterly may not recover their fluency in that first tongue until they hear it spoken around them. Experiments have shown that material learned in one class-room is more fully recalled in the same place than in a different class-room, and even paired syllables are relearned more rapidly if presented on the same coloured background on both occasions than if the colour is changed for relearning. Internal as well as external cues can serve as mediators, so that the relearning of nonsense syllables is more efficient if the subject adopts the same body posture on both occasions than it is if he changes, for example, from erect position to supine. External or internal cues are the more helpful the more marginal the success in recall and performance may fail because of an inability to perceive such cues.

Retrieval strategies

Insofar as recall is the end product of a search process, its accuracy and extent depend on the completion of that process. With highly practised skills or much-rehearsed data, little search is needed and the probability of successful recall is high. Once we have learned to write we are unlikely to be at a loss as to how to grip a pen and after some practice on the typewriter the need to search for a key is the exception rather than the rule. We can name our present address quite promptly, but may require some time to name an earlier one that was as readily accessible at that date as is our current address now. We can repeat the latest news in considerable detail and with fair fidelity to the report we have read or heard, but are unlikely to reconstruct yesterday's quite so well even with a good deal more effort and have little chance of recapturing last week's. Whether this is so because traces decay over time, or are overlaid and the content is pushed into more remote files, the signal to noise ratio of this type of information progressively contracts over time.

The lower the signal property of a memory, the less likely it is to be retrieved in search or the longer the search required to retrieve it. There is always a chance probability of hitting on it early in the search process, as there is of giving up the search before reaching its goal. Yet another possibility is a premature termination of the search with an incorrect or partly correct response which is mistaken for the correct one. Failure in matching the content of recall to the object of the search process is, theoretically, a source of failure independent of the inaccessibility of its storage. Signal detection theory has sorted out two components that contribute to errors in recognition or matching. One is a defect in discrimination, an inability to perceive distinctive cues, as happens when we mistake a child for his identical twin. Another cause of inaccurate recognition is the adoption of lax standards of discrimination. Some people regularly accept more lenient criteria of identity or of truth than others and everybody tends to apply more stringent criteria in certain situations, for the type of data that are especially significant to him. One is more willing to drink from a bottle that bears a label dimly reminiscent of a delectable wine than from a bottle that looks equally reminiscent of a medicine that once relieved a crippling intestinal cramp.

Whenever rigorous criteria of identity are in force, the search process is likely to be more exhaustive and to conclude with a response of 'don't know' rather than with an incorrect answer. There are several possible search strategies and the most effective keep down the load of information needed for progress, and eliminate duplications. Failure of recall very often results from a perseveration with an incorrect response, an apparent inability to direct the beam away from that unpromising spot. Inefficient search strategies create more recall interference than the efficient and also produce less enrichment generated by the search process. For it is evident in many instances of recall that related and relevant content accrues to the information sought in the process of search.

4 Biological Models of Memory and Learning

The changes in behaviour manifested in learning, the registration, storage and retrieval of memories all arise in the brain. Most psychological theories of learning and remembering have been formulated with a brain model in sight. This respect shown to the laws and mechanisms of the neural sciences may have guarded psychological speculation from flights into fancy but has hardly endowed it with rich factual material. While a great deal is known about the behavioural and experiential aspects of learning and remembering, the neurophysiological processes involved are far from clearly understood and the neuropathology associated with disordered function is quite patchy. The most valuable lessons learned from the neural sciences are those which invalidate certain theories of learning and remembering. It is incompatible with current neuropathological data that learning and remembering should be subserved by one specific, however large, area of the brain; it is improbable that memories should be represented uniquely in any one site of the brain; and from Penfield's (1954) observations of epileptic patients it seems likely 'that the mechanism of recall or memory is anatomically separated from the mechanism of recording.'

Neuroanatomical Models

Biological theories of learning and remembering divide into two general classes. One is the product of the clinical laboratory, and of the venerable scientific endeavour to map parallels between bodily and mental functions. Its goal is to isolate the sites in the brain that are involved in the processes of learning and remembering, damage to which results in impaired learning and memory. The other approach is less concerned with anatomical areas than with the electrophysiological and chemical properties of the brain, and attempts to reconstruct from these data a working model of cerebral function. The contributions to the latter theories have come chiefly from the neurophysiological and neurochemical laboratories, with supporting observations on experimentally controlled animal performance.

Limbic system

Most of the anatomical information has been obtained by post-mortem examination of the brains of patients known to have had severe memory or learning disorders. The majority of these studies implicates one or another site on a functionally continuous neural circuit, the *limbic system*, that involves the cingulate cortex, hippocampus, fornix, hypothalamus, mammillothalamic tract and thalamus. More especially, the mammillary bodies have been found to be damaged in a large number of cases but similar psychological defects are also associated with lesions in the medial dorsal thalamus and with bilateral ablation of the hippocampus, if the tissue involved extends a given distance beyond uncus and amygdala.

Only the effects of temporal lobectomy can be evaluated with the precision and control afforded by a surgical procedure. Of the several sites listed, the fornix has been transected operatively in a number of patients but reports of consequent defects in learning and memory form the exception rather than the rule. The dorsal medial thalamus has also been subjected to partial extirpation by stereotaxic surgery, for example, in order to relieve otherwise intractable pain, but there is only the most tentative evidence of learning or memory impairment in patients who underwent such operations. Brain damage in the mammillary bodies as well as in most other areas implicated in the amnesic syndrome has been caused either by degenerative changes, by vascular accidents, by inflammatory diseases or by the pressure of tumours. In one patient, a case reported by Rizzo (1955), the memory and other psychological disturbances characteristic of the Korsakoff syndrome developed with the growth of a haematic cyst and disappeared with its recession. The patient died within a year of his recovery from a lung disease and autopsy revealed an empty cyst adjoining the mammillary bodies.

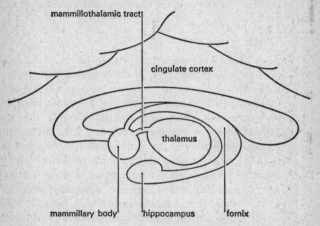

Figure 3 Brain centres implicated in memory disorders

In most other instances the pathological record of the cerebral damage associated with the onset of a memory disorder becomes obscured during the interval that precedes autopsy, and even in instances of surgical exposure of the brain it is often difficult to determine how much tissue may have been damaged indirectly and in what cerebral regions or systems.

Ablation experiments with animals allow for the exact demarcation of cerebral areas as well as for accurate comparisons of pre-operative and post-operative performance. Their lesions, however, have only a limited applicability to human learning and even less to those operations in remembering that seem unique to man. It is significant that the limbic system, implicated in severe memory dis-

turbances, is involved principally in the emotional behaviour of subhuman species. The gulf between the two
sets of observations is not unbridgeable, since most clinical
reports about severely amnesic patients also mention
anomalies in affect and particularly in spontaneity. There
is some indication that the relative contribution of the
latter symptoms and of the amnesic derangement may
vary according to the site of the lesion in the limbic
system but the observations available to date do not allow
for any definitive conclusion.

Functional maps of the brain

In fact the neuroanatomical evidence is strongest where it
rules out certain hypotheses. Except for verbal messages,
information is not recorded in one hemisphere but probably duplicated in the mirror position of the other hemisphere and very likely in several additional sites or nets
of the brain as well. Cerebral systems necessary for learning, for the transfer of information into permanent
storage, are not depositories of memories and may not be
necessary for recapturing old memories. The hippocampus, by modulating reticular and thalamic neural patterns,
seems to serve the function of investing incoming messages with significance and assigning their place in the
memory files, of embedding them in the matrix of pre-
established records. Whether any such hypothetical function also involves the recoding processes necessary for
registration is entirely beyond verification in our present
state of knowledge; nor can we determine the extent to
which the other functionally related brain areas are necessary for these operations. They, or some of them, are quite
apparently involved in those intentional processes by
which plans are set up and in the sequencing operations
by which they are executed. The plans that require an
intact mammillothalamic-fornix system comprise all
types of sustained and goal-directed behaviour, other than
those which are propelled by sensory feedback or physiological drives or overlearned skills and habits, and include

the registration of information as well as the search for and recovery of memories.

Although the content of learning and of remembering may be of the highest order and complexity, the phylogenetically older and architectonically inferior divisions of the brain are as necessary for executing the required operations as is the cortex. Disorders of learning and memory have been reported in many patients with indisputable lesions in the limbic system. The case for similar derangements associated with exclusively cortical lesions is much weaker; it has been put forward perhaps more forcefully on *a priori* grounds than on those of empirical observations, and in either case seems tenable only on the assumption of diffuse rather than focal damage.

Neurochemical Models

The structural changes that could occur in the brain as a result of learning and that would break down when something is forgotten have been conceived both in anatomical and in chemical terms. Anatomical changes that are thought to correspond to new learning are at the cellular or neuronal level. Biochemical changes have recently been formulated at the molecular level. Anatomical models typically focus on the synapse, the junction between any two neurons, and on the thousands of dendrites by which each neuron enters into synaptic connexions. These synapses are modifiable; they grow knobs; their power can be increased by repetitive activation and thus they provide an ideal medium for long-term retention primed by a transitory process of information storage. The synaptic model of structural memory allows for growth with experience in spite of the fact that the number of brain cells available over a life span is determined at birth and progressively declines. This model does not depend on the hypothesis of qualitative differences in neurons or indeed on the assumption that information is stored in single neurons. It does not run counter to the empirical laws of the neural sciences and admits a fairly direct translation into computer hardware. All it needs is some proof that learning and forgetting are accompanied by predictable changes in synaptic structure or function.

Whether learning is subserved by neural growth or by changes in synaptic transmission, it involves some biochemical processes either at the stage of acquisition or in storage, or in both. There has been considerable interest in the part played by acetylcholine, the agent released in the process of synaptic transmission, and in cholinesterase, the enzyme that neutralizes it, and some indication from animal experiments that chemicals inhibiting one or the other exert differential effects on newly acquired and on established habits. Following the discovery of the part played by D N A in storing genetic information, there has been extensive speculation and experimentation on the possible biochemical mechanism by which information acquired through experience is stored. 'These proposals have considered such reactions as nucleic acid synthesis, protein synthesis, enzyme induction, and antibody formation as possible models for the biological basis of this process.' Barondes (1965), the author quoted, adds that the neurochemical theories of learning and memory are founded on a self-evident proposition, assuming that the biological regulatory mechanisms of the organism must also operate in the central nervous system to mediate information storage. His interest is in the part protein molecules play in the development of new synaptic connexions. Other investigators are more interested in the protein molecule as the physical trace, varying in structure according to the content of the memory it encodes.

Molecular basis of storage

The theory that memory traces are formed by the rearrangement of the molecular structure in a nerve cell goes back at least to Delboeuf (1876) who proposed it almost a century ago. Experiments have since shown that the structure of protein molecules is subject to change, especially under the impact of electrical impulses travelling in nerve fibres. The resulting new structures, however, are short lived and could not serve as the biological storage mechanism of lasting memories. They are, however, capable of reproducing themselves in an interminable sequence of replicates, by means of templates provided by RNA (ribonucleic acid) molecules. According to the theory, each replicate modulates the release of the synaptic transmitter agent so as to reproduce the pattern of electrical impulses associated with new learning. Hydén (1965), the champion of the theory that learning is accomplished by the production and release of distinctive RNA molecules, and consequently by distinctive protein molecules, has, along with his followers, done extensive research to demonstrate the importance of RNA in learning and retention. They have observed changes in neuronal RNA during conditioning in experimental animals that could indicate an increased rate of RNA synthesis. Animal experiments have shown that pharmacological inhibition of neuronal protein synthesis impairs the retention of conditioned responses and may indeed prevent the transfer of learning from a temporary to a stable storage system. There have been reports of improved learning in patients with memory disorders after oral or intravenous administration of RNA or of a drug that is alleged to promote RNA synthesis in the brain, and also of favourable learning effects in animals as a result of similar treatment.

Most puzzling of all experiments in this field are those that feed trained animals or their brains to untrained representatives of the same species and show that this 'cannibalistic' procedure speeds up learning, and that moreover its facilitating effects are quite specific to the learning task on which the victim was trained. In view of the numerous negative results in similar experiments, the evidence for the chemical transmission of learned responses between different members of a species is far from conclusive and even if it were so it would allow for more than one interpretation. The same observation applies to all experiments conducted to test the role of R N A in learning and remembering. Most investigators have failed to improve the performance of patients with memory disorders by giving them R N A or drugs that are thought to stimulate R N A synthesis. Experiments designed to interfere with protein synthesis in the brain indicate that R N A may only serve in transferring information to protein molecules rather than in coding it or indeed that the messenger R N A involved in information storage must be available prior to new learning. Furthermore, as Cohen, Barondes and Ervin (1966) have shown, such antibiotic agents as inhibit protein synthesis may interfere with learning or retention, not by means of a direct chemical effect but through disrupting the normal electrical activity of the brain.

The experimental findings available to date, apart from being far removed from the operations typical of human learning and remembering, are controversial and the attribution of the positive results to the role of R N A or protein molecules is somewhat arbitrary. From the psychological point of view the real difficulty lies in the attempt to break down all learning and experience into elementary units or memories, each of which could be coded in a different molecule.

Synaptic changes in learning

Perhaps this problem is not so insurmountable in neurochemical analyses of the mechanisms of learning and information storage that are geared to a model of synaptic changes in which a specific memory is determined, not by one, but by any number of sites along a neural pathway and by their sequential order of firing. Examples of dissociative or 'state-dependent' learning in which animals trained under a drug could display a conditioned response only if again injected with that drug may be quoted in support of this brain model of learning. The drug could, of course, serve merely as a potent cue, somewhat like Proust's madeleine.

Another conditioning experiment combined with injection, however, produced evidence against the hypothesis that information is stored by means of synaptic changes along specific neural pathways in the brain. In one of his experiments exploring the conditions by which learning is transferred from the active to the depressed hemisphere of the brain (cf. p. 58), Albert (1966b) removed a rat's medial cortex. After this operation, the rat was unable to perform the conditioned response even though both hemispheres were functioning normally. Retraining could, however, be speeded up by intraperitoneal injection of the removed and homogenized brain tissue. This effect could be observed only if the operation was delayed for several hours after the original training (more evidence for consolidation) and was entirely absent if the tissue injected came from other brain sites or from the excised area of another animal – evidence against cannibalism as a technique to improve learning. The positive results of this experiment are certainly incompatible with the hypothesis that the chemical changes that subserve learning occur in specific synapses or nerve cells, since it is quite improbable that the injected tissue would find its way to such sites in the originally depressed hemisphere.

Current biochemical models of learning and of information storage would appear to have assumed a significance far beyond that warranted by the tentative conclusions of largely contradictory experiments. This is due in part to the expectancy of a decisive breakthrough and especially to the hope of discovering effective pharmacological agents for the control of performance and the remedying of defects. Just as pharmacological treatment has offered the most powerful means to relieve the symptoms of and to control disordered behaviour in mental diseases, it is widely expected that they will also benefit mankind by correcting learning defects and failing memories. If they will, we can only increase our gains by knowing how they achieve those effects.

Neurophysiological Models

Neuroanatomical theories of learning and memory entail
a neurophysiological explantion, for they assume that the
damage in a site crucial to these functions interrupts a
cerebral activity. In so far as the hippocampal–fornix–
mammillary system is most often implicated in memory
disorders, it is believed that it constitutes a pathway to
whatever storage sites there may be in the brain. A close
and stable correspondence between cerebral structure and
function is predicated both on *a priori* grounds and supported by empirical data obtained from clinical studies
and from animal experiments using ablation and stimulation techniques. There is reason to doubt though that this
correspondence is as close in the intact as in the damaged
brain, in the wakeful as in the anaesthetized animal.

Neurophysiological models of learning and memory,
though they be couched in terms of some degree of localization of brain function, need not imply structural
changes. They can be formulated on the assumption that
the elements of the brain remain constant and unchanged
and that learning and remembering are accomplished by
the functional reorganization of these elements. Neurophysiological theories are concerned primarily with the
functional properties of neural systems, of networks as
well as single neurons, tracts and nuclei. The experimentally established constraints on these systems also
serve as clues to their likely function. Their basic unit is
the neuron which is either at rest or firing, carries messages
in one direction only and transmits them to an adjacent
neuron across a synapse. Neurons are not all at rest in the
absence of synaptic excitation and therefore the effect of
an external event impinging on a sense organ or of a
neuronal impulse traversing the synapse is to modify a pre-
existing state. The impulse generated by a single neuron
is thought to be insufficient to transmit information,
although its repetitive impact on, for example, the same
synaptic knob could result in cumulative and enduring

physiological or anatomical changes that would subserve lasting memory.

There is reason to believe that learning, even at the level of conditioning, involves neural aggregates, that is, large populations of nerve cells, rather than one or a few neurons or a single neural pathway. Contrary to the hypotheses basic to Pavlovian conditioning theory, functional systems in the brain are arranged in columns perpendicular to rather than in nets on the surface of the cortex. It would therefore be logically indicated to record electrophysiological activity in depth along such columns, whereas for practical reasons the standard technique of such recordings is based on samples of surface neurons. Even so, uniform patterns of spontaneous or evoked firing can be indicative of the cerebral organization by which information is processed, recorded and retrieved, more especially of organization at sub-cortical levels. According to John (1965), during conditioning 'extensive neural regions acquire an invariant component of response' and he also quotes experiments showing that, in the process of information retrieval, the same patterns of electrical activity reappear in several sites of the brain.

Planning and sequencing

An assumption that underlies the neurophysiological models is that the cortex is only partly pre-wired, that is, that only some of its neural aggregates are involved in specific, for example, sensory or motor, functions while others are equipotentially available for the establishment of learnt behaviour, whether in the form of unique pathways or of unique spatio-temporal patterns of firing. Any number of reasons can, of course, be listed why these originally non-specific neural systems should be less than normally available to those who are handicapped by disorders of learning and remembering. One of the most likely defects is in a neural system that keeps up searching operations until the information sought in recall has been found, as well as other planning and sequencing operations in behaviour. This is Pribram's (1958) frontal intrinsic system which abounds in homeostatic mechanisms at its core, a neural system that has both functional unity and anatomical identity and includes the several nuclei and tracts known to be impaired in amnesic syndromes.

The proposition that certain gross disorders of memory are in fact one of several associated manifestations of an underlying disturbance in a general programming function or in vigilance does not exclude the existence of exclusive or specific memory disorders, of disabilities limited to the acquisition or retrieval of information by means of one sensory modality. Neither does it solve the problem of information storage, but it agrees with the notion that neurons must be sensitized in certain combinations in order to establish a lasting record or to read out such a record. The record itself, whether formed by a network of brain cells or, as appears more likely, by a spatio-temporal pattern among anatomically separated neural units, can be damaged. Another possible source of memory defect might lie in faulty matching operations, impaired recognition. The capacity to retrieve records could be sufficient and the records could be intact and yet the information extracted would be incorrect.

Computer models

Since the neural mechanisms and processes involved in the registration, storage and retrieval of information are not known, analogies drawn from computer operations have been extensively used for electrophysiological models. At first these analogies were rather more specific than was warranted by the facts known, for example, between relays and synapses or between wiring in the hardware and neural networks. Recently, the analogy has been based more on the general consideration that computers, like the brain, are information processing devices; they code, store and combine information in logical patterns far more effectively than any other known machine.

The computer provides an ideal tool for simulating brain models conceived in terms of digital logic, as it does for analysing electrophysiological data monitored from a real brain. For the study of memory it has the virtue of being liable to deranged functioning without the use of drugs or the imposition of lesions. Even if in due course it should be superseded by some other hardware model of brain function, the computer analogy will have done valuable service by stimulating speculation about memory processes and mechanisms that operate as statistically organized systems and are not tied to fixed neural pathways. It has also helped to extend the theoretical analyses from an exclusive preoccupation with problems of storage to a concern for those presented by information input and retrieval. For in the computer, information, unless it is properly programmed for access, will not be available on demand and a faultless system of memory storage is of no avail if the retrieval programme is defective.

5 Motivated Breakdown of Memory and Learning

Normal Breakdown in the Mechanisms of Registration, Search and Correction

All models of learning and remembering, psychological or biological, furnish some entirely sufficient reasons for failures in performance, for complete forgetting or partially correct recall. Indeed the lawful incidence of defects in learning and remembering provides the best clues as to how these processes might operate when intact. Most of those defects occur in normal as well as in pathological function, so that a distinction between the two is justified in quantitative as well as in qualitative terms.

There are occasions in everyone's life when he cannot learn with any lasting effect. The most obvious instances are those in which the load exceeds normal capacity; there is just too much to learn, or too little time available, or the foundations in previous learning are insufficient for assimilating a difficult or complex skill or piece of information. Many actresses may never succeed in mastering the role of Shakespeare's Cleopatra and some may need longer to learn it than others, but none is likely to choose this part for her first stage appearance. One can fail to learn something well within one's capacity on an off day or while preoccupied with other matters, under emotional stress or in a state of fatigue. All these and similar unfavourable circumstances could be bracketed under the heading of insufficient attention and would also account for unsuccessful attempts at recall.

Search and substitution

Someone who is tired at the end of a hard day is quite apt to fail in his attempt to exercise a well-established skill or to find some known item of information. The response that seems unavailable to him is so because he cannot complete the searching operations necessary to reach it. He may substitute the wrong response, either because the situation demands some response, for example a facetious or evasive comment in lieu of an informative answer, or because he does not realize that his response is incorrect. The circumstances that cut short his search operations also impair his self-correcting mechanisms.

Errors of memory by incorrect substitution, especially those that can be observed in psychopathological instances, suggest that whenever we have to find a specific memory any number of responses become available. The alcohol addict's propensity to furnish inexact information, the so-called positive symptoms of amnesic disorders attest to a breakdown in some inhibitory mechanism. Normally, we arrive at our answers by a process of selection, by eliminating those candidates that do not fit one or another of our criteria of correctness. This seems a most uneconomical process and time consuming but there is no reason why our brains should not be capable of performing it by following a hierarchical logical model rapidly enough to produce an instantaneous response. With much practised skills or messages the search, of course, can be quite short and the effect of overlearning is that the proper response will always appear first and be passed with a minimal check of its fit.

That such checking and fitting often precedes correct recall is apparent from trials to place a memory in its proper context. An example familiar to everyone is the search undertaken to locate the source of a quotation or of a few bars of music. The same circumstances that favour erroneous substitutions also encourage errors of memory by contextual misplacement and false denials. Especially common is the denial of previous knowledge when in fact only a denial of access would be true. That the problem is one of search can be demonstrated by aiding the tired person to find the required piece of information. It is also evident from the difficulties one has in hitting on the right phrase or word to convey the intended meaning of a message.

Motivated forgetting

A lack of capacity to retrieve the information required or to sift out the incorrect data is not the only cause of normal errors in memory. Much forgetting can be attributed to motivational determinants. Memories that would cause pain, discomfort, insults to one's self-esteem or threats to one's values, are apt to be forgotten. Most of us have but the haziest recollections of painful accidents or of such threats to our lives as we clearly became aware of in an air raid or in a hair-breadth escape of a collision on the highway. If many people tend to brood over insults received and setbacks, others seem to forget completely quite unmistakable rebuffs to their attempts at self-assertion, or incontrovertible arguments marshalled against their cherished ideas. Experimental studies have demonstrated the superior recall as well as learning of controversial statements that confirm one's prejudices or opinions over statements that conflict with them.

Repression

Of all motivational influences on memory, forgetting through repression has received most attention. Broadly defined, repression refers to the inaccessibility of memories which, if recalled, or of skills which, if executed, would cause pain or arouse anxiety. The term is derived from psychoanalytic theory and at first served Freud (1900, 1953) to cover all defence mechanisms. Later Freud (1925, 1929) ear-marked it as one of several such unconscious mechanisms, more particularly as the mechanism that keeps out of consciousness ideas associated in childhood with sexual and aggressive impulses, ideas that would arouse anxiety if admitted into consciousness. Like extinction in conditioning theory, repression is not so much an example of forgetting as a type of learning, learning not to remember some event or theme, some verbal or other response.

Repressed content cannot, by definition, be recalled at will. Its retention is inferred from dreams or from certain anomalies in behaviour, especially verbal behaviour. There are also special techniques, for example, free association, as understood by psychoanalysts, and hypnosis, by which repressed material can be brought to the surface of consciousness. Hypnosis also furnishes another example of the process by which the content of memories is barred from recall, and is so without motivational reasons. Observations made and actions carried out under hynosis are not remembered unless the hypnotist orders their recall. He may also instruct his subject to say or do something at a given time or on arbitrarily selected cues when he is no longer in a hypnotic trance and the subject will act in obedience to this post-hypnotic suggestion without recollecting the instruction or, indeed, without any idea why he should be acting in the prescribed manner.

Whether interpreted narrowly or broadly, repression would seem to be a most valuable constituent of ordered function, an adjuvant in learning and in effective remembering. It represents one of the selective processes by which memories are placed outside the limits of normal access. It is not the only source of forgetting but – allowing for a broad definition – it is an important source. Experiments conducted to demonstrate repression have produced results that are consistent with the theory but not quite sufficient to confirm it. Probably the first of these experiments was Jung and Riklin's (1904) word association technique. This method consists of presenting the subject with a list of words after instructing him to respond as rapidly as he can to each with the first word that comes to his mind. Long latencies, silence and hesitation are all taken as indicative of 'complexes'.

Repression in normal function

Like complexes, repression operates in normal as well as in

psychiatrically disturbed persons. One of Freud's (1960) best-known books was written to illustrate the effects of repression in such instances in everyday life as lapses of memory and slips of the tongue. Regarding the former, the evidence for motivation is quite convincing in some instances, and excessively laboured in others. It seems perfectly justified to conclude that repression accounts for some lapses of memory but others, perhaps the majority, are attributable to entirely unmotivated sources.

Repression is even less powerful as a universal explanation of slips of the tongue. To be sure, the substitution of opposites or of words that differ in one letter but carry completely different meanings often produces quite amusing effects and sometimes may indeed betray secret thoughts or even unconscious desires, but far more often it remains unnoticed, precisely because no such hidden purpose can be construed from the error. If one accepts the view that we store our vocabularies, as we do all information, in some systematic fashion, it follows that opposites are filed quite close one to the other and, in a different system, so are words that sound or look alike. If there is a failure in the process of recall and if it is corrected by substitution, it is obvious that – next to synonyms – antonyms, homonyms and other words similar in form or meaning would be chosen most frequently. The criteria of similarity can be more or less universal or quite idiosyncratic.

Repression also serves in psychoanalytic theory to explain the fact that most of our early childhood experiences are forgotten and normally inaccessible to recall. If, as has been argued, these experiences are remembered in dreams, in hypnosis, in free association, then the psychoanalytic thesis rests on quite strong arguments, but the evidence is hardly of a kind that passes the criterion of unbiased observation. Far more plausible is the explanation that memories must be registered in the first place and that registration presupposes some pre-existing categories of information filing. The formation of such categories takes time and varied experience. It begins with attempts in perceptual discrimination, proceeds through trials in testing the validity of those discriminations and then through similar operations at the conceptual level. It would indeed be surprising if a child under three years were to be in command of all the classificatory system that is necessary for the registration of even the most common experiences and observations.

Hysteric repression

If repression affected only memories that would arouse irrational anxiety and none of the learning that is necessary to avert genuine danger, it would hardly qualify as a source of disordered function. Psychoanalytic theory does not hold that repression in fact extends to such learning, but it does teach that repression prevents people from facing certain real-life tests and thus from learning to adapt to those situations. It also implies that repression need not be complete and that the residual 'forces' barred from consciousness will seek an alternative outlet in symptom formation. Moreover, repression is apt to become a general trait of memory function and thus to restrict available information. This trait is especially characteristic of hysterical persons, in whom it operates according to predictable or recognizable rules, more particularly in accordance with some themes or content areas.

The mechanism and the effects of repression are less easily predicted than reconstructed from a knowledge of the person who resorts to them. This is so because the content and pattern of repression vary widely among different persons. The effects of repression also differ in their intensity, so that in some people they merely determine their personalities, in others they build up into psychoneurotic symptoms and in others they interfere with the discharge of normal social responsibilities. Regarding the variety of symptoms manifested by psychiatric patients it would be difficult to improve on Hunter's (1957) exhaustive inventory. 'It may be the recollection of all experiences related to a certain event or sphere of activity. It may be only a name, or a word, or a phrase. And it may not only be the recollection but also the recall (performance) of definite motor habits such as how to write, or sew, or drive a car, or make a bed. The patient may even forget how to stand or walk, although he has not lost the ability to use his legs in other ways. In short, repressing may involve the blocking off of any experience or learned performance and the resulting loss may be either slight or extensive' (rev. edn, p. 236).

The basic rule of repression is the isolation of a system of learnt behaviour or memories and its functional dissociation from other systems. It is a characteristic sign of hysteric patients who are also notorious for developing conversion symptoms, for example, paralyses, anaesthesias, that is, the blocking of a circumscribed set of afferent or efferent messages without structural damage in the nervous system. Hysteric patients have provided many of the observations on which Freud based his psychological theory and have been notable for their responsiveness to psychoanalytic treatment.

Examples of hysteric repression are copious and two incidents related by colleagues of mine will illustrate the phenomenon. One concerns a young woman who, shortly after starting psychoanalytic treatment, came across her psychiatrist at a theatre which he attended in his wife's company. Doctor and patient acknowledged each other's presence. Treatment continued without any reference to that encounter. Since, however, by the rules of psychoanalytic procedure, the patient was supposed to discuss all significant experiences, it soon became apparent that she had no recollection whatever of going to the theatre or of the play she saw. She had some vague memory of being driven to the theatre and later driving home, but none of the intervening experiences. Naturally enough the observations made during that period were not completely erased and, in due course, some memory of the theatre and play emerged, although this memory still appeared to be inordinately poor in content and entirely excluded the figure of the psychiatrist.

My other informant recalled a patient of his early practice, with whom he had made little headway over the weeks, until suddenly one day she began to pour out the type of material that, according to the textbooks, should emerge in psychotherapy. The young psychiatrist felt he had at last broken through a barrier and wrote extensive notes of the interview. One can well imagine his discouragement when two days later he received a telephone call from the patient apologizing for missing her last appointment. Somehow, she confessed, the matter had completely slipped her mind and she could not even remember what she was doing at the time she should have gone to his office. It was not a temporary amnesia for the incident, for she never again found her way to those gates that had been opened up in that isolated interview.

These instances of isolating memory of a particular event would be less puzzling if the event had taken place in a very unusual geographic and social setting, where the patient's habitual behaviour were entirely inappropriate. In actual fact, her behaviour is quite normal and conventional. She finds her way to and from the site, relates to the persons and objects in her usual manner and exercises her social and linguistic skills with customary efficiency. All these learnt behaviour patterns transferred from earlier situations and reapplied subsequently, however, seem completely ineffective as an avenue for recall. Even the temporally contiguous memories dissolve as they approach the boundaries of the isolated episode, as dreams are prone to terminate abruptly the moment the cherished goal comes within reach.

It does seem as if the isolated experience were hedged by impenetrable barriers especially raised for the purpose and set across the lines of all the usual paths of access. This is just another way to describe the mechanism of repression, for there can be little doubt that the barriers are raised to protect the person from some experience, some memory or thought about the future, that would shatter his hope or self-image. The occasions or motives of repression, however, tell us nothing about the mechanism by which the defensive operation is accomplished. This could be an exceedingly rapid feed-back system in the brain which, in hysteric persons, functions with particular efficiency, possibly because – as a result of an innate disposition, or of learning, or both – they are better able than other people to structure their experiences into self-contained sub-systems. They can turn upon their schemata, as Bartlett (1932) suggested we do when we recall memories from our past, and also turn away rapidly. Eysenck's (1957) theory, according to which hysterical persons are endowed with an exceptionally strong inhibitory potential, would account for the efficiency of their repressive mechanism.

Multiple personalities

Memories in permanent storage are organized in systems according to various co-ordinating or hierarchical principles. If asked to recount the events of last week, one memory will lead to another through temporal contiguity but, if one of those incidents happened to be a medical examination, it is quite feasible to strike out into another direction and list the various doctors one has visited at different times in the past and in different places. For many people the past has but little temporal organization and Paul (1959) holds that this is particularly characteristic of hysterical persons. Bleuler (1924) thought that even the apparent temporal circumscription of hysteric amnesias is in fact determined by content. The part played by temporal organization in memory function, and the breakdown of that organization, will be considered in chapter 7. It is clearly not the only principle of organization of past experiences, for we accumulate knowledge and relate facts, whether of our personal or impersonal lives, with other facts in any number of diverse patterns. This is implied in the statement that we learn by association, a statement that also predicates a second law, namely, that our associations follow certain learnt rules alike in the acquisition and the recollection of information.

These rules can admit almost any degree of complexity and comprehensiveness. Indeed, only a consistent application of a rule can explain the formation, maintenance and development of such a complicated construction as the experiential person or self. This is evident from the reports of the psychopathological phenomena that occur in multiple personalities, fugue states and loss of personal identity. There are records of people who functioned alternately as two or more virtually distinct personalities, each differing from the others by characteristic traits, interests and life experience. These personalities that dwell in the same body are known as alternating personalities and they can be co-conscious, one-way amnesic, or mutually amnesic, according to the awareness of each personality of the current and past conduct of the alternate. The memories of each can be so organized that no communication takes place between it and another or all of the alternating personalities. In somnambulism, for example, the somnambulistic personality is completely unaware of the actions and thoughts of its normal alternate.

Alternate personalities are usually quite unlike one another; they differ in temperament, values and social attitudes, standards of conduct, and may do so even in respect to age and sex. In spite of these differences and of the barriers between their memories of the personal past, which may or may not be lifted under hypnosis or other psychiatric treatment, the alternate personalities share a good deal of learning, their command of the vocabulary and of the grammatical rules being possibly the most conspicuous examples, although a free access to profanities may be limited to only one of them.

The mechanism by which such 'co-conscious' personalities are sustained within the same organism is quite obscure and the more so as typically one or more of the multiple personalities has been brought into observable existence by hypnosis or other manipulative techniques that are not clearly understood. The phenomenon of multiple personalities has been interpreted as an intense version of role playing in which the actor cannot divest himself of his assumed character at will. This model is most plausible whenever the secondary personality corresponds to a long cherished ideal built up in fantasy or affords an outlet for aspirations and impulses that would remain repressed or suppressed in the primary personality. The rigid separation of personalities and frequent lack of communication between them, however, remain unexplained by the role theory. Multiple personalities, nevertheless, serve well to illustrate the comprehensive and exclusive principles by which memory systems are organized, even though they cast little light on these processes of organization.

Fugue state and loss of personal identity

The related psychopathological phenomena of fugue states and loss of personal identity are perhaps more informative, in that they furnish immediate evidence for the influence exerted by intense emotions on the organization of experiences and memories. In fugue states the person affected loses his personal identity, including all personal memories, and typically assuming a new identity, embarks on a completely new life. He may leave his home town and settle elsewhere, start an entirely new job, forget about his previous work as well as about his family, friends and other personal relationships, possessions, and interests. To all appearances, at least in the eyes of those who did not know him, he acts and behaves normally until one day – and that may be after several years – he recovers his old personal identity. Fugue states can terminate in a loss of personal identity, a disturbance which also occurs independently and differs from fugues in that the person affected is aware of the fact that he does not know who he is, where he comes from, etc. Both conditions are followed by total amnesia for the period over which they prevailed, and have been shown to be precipitated as well as terminated by emotional stress or shock. The emotional upheaval may, but does not necessarily, follow such manifest insults as shell shock or epileptic seizure, witnessing a scene of intense suffering, or receiving extremely painful news.

A much quoted example of major memory disturbance unambiguously precipitated by a severe emotional upheaval is Janet's (1920) patient, Irène. In her case the derangement stopped short of a loss of personal identity but was clearly the product of quite similar dissociative processes. Irène had nursed her mother through the terminal stages of consumption – a twenty-year-old girl forced to be the witness of a slow and particularly painful process of dying in a squalid attic. The circumstances of that period of agony, the girl's attempts to revive the corpse and then to lift the inert body to the bed, were recalled by Irène and also re-enacted with the liveliness and accuracy of a dramatic performance in repeated spells that Janet described as somnambulisms. Often the faithful resuscitation of the past would be embellished by hallucinatory dialogues and actions. Following her mother's death Irène would make preparations for her suicide. She would stretch out on the floor waiting to be run over by a train and as 'the train arrives before her staring eyes, she utters a terrible shriek, and falls back motionless, as if she were dead. She soon gets up and begins acting over again one of the preceding scenes.'

Between these 'somnambulist' attacks, Irène's behaviour was remarkable for its insensitiveness. She appeared to have forgotten her mother's death and the illness that had preceded it. Rationally she was willing to accept the fact that her mother had died, since she could not see her around and was herself in mourning, but remembered neither the date nor the cause of her death and wondered why she had not taken care of her while she had been so ill. Irène was also astonished: 'Why, loving her as I did, do I not feel more sorrow for her death?' In her 'normal' condition, Irène was as incapable of re-experiencing her feelings toward her mother as of recalling the episodes or general circumstances that surrounded her final agony. Whether Irène's amnesia can be explained by the pain of the memory exceeding the threshold of toleration or, as McDougall (1926) thought, by 'rebellious impulses' aroused by the 'desires for companionship and gaiety, and perhaps for a lover', impulses that she had to repress while nursing her mother and that may have given rise to fantasies, it was unquestionably an affectively determined disorder.

There are also obvious parallels between Irène's 'normal' self alternating with 'somnambulist' fits and the alteration of multiple personalities. In the other direction parallels can be drawn between her and patients who in their seizures lapse into a cataleptic trance. All these dissociative derangements have been attributed to motivational–affective influences, and more particularly to repression. Repression very satisfactorily accounts for the seemingly complete oblivion of intolerable injuries and insults suffered under duress and of all kinds of events and facts related to these by contiguity or by causal connexion. It is more debatable whether global amnesias, such as those observed in the Korsakoff syndrome, have ever been produced by repression or indeed whether emotional factors play an important part in all memory disorders.

In the literature there are any number of telling examples that illustrate the influence of affective factors on the occasions and content of amnesias and on the occasions of recovery and the content recovered from amnesias. These examples support the case for emotional determinants of memory and memory disorders but do not justify the argument often implied, often explicitly stated, that emotional determinants can be detected in all memory disorders. Careful students of several different types of memory disturbances have reported observations that directly conflict with such a general law. Affective determinants of memory disorders are invariably found in

hysteric personalities, persons who are particularly subject
to repression and denial. Multiple personalities, fugue
states, loss of personal identity are all typically hysterical
manifestations. The misperception of the sensory environment and false reconstruction of past experiences in accordance with a dominant affect, however, are not unique to
hysteric persons. These anomalies can occur in the midst
of a diffuse amnesic disturbance, as I observed (Talland,
1965) in a woman whose Korsakoff syndrome was unambiguously related to alcohol and who very likely had a
hysteric personality, and in a man who probably did not
and whose amnesic syndrome and virtually total dementia
originated in an encephalitis. Neither of those patients
mistook his personal identity, but both were thoroughly
confused about members of their families and persons in
their immediate surrounding, as well as about past personal experiences.

Post-traumatic psychogenic amnesia

Faced with the observations that demonstrable insults to
the brain and severely disturbing experiences – physical
or emotional traumata – can produce the same psychological, for example amnesic, disorders, it has been proposed that physical traumata provide occasions for the
emergence of hysterical reactions. This thesis has been
supported by the many war-time victims of shell shock
who had lost their personal identity or had wandered
behind the front line in a fugue state. Typically, they
were in a state of amnesia for the traumatic incident
which, however, many could reconstruct under hypnosis.
Among the reports in the literature there is one by Syz
(1937), notable for its systematic investigation and follow-up of a patient whose traumatic amnesia developed
into a chronic, albeit reversible, memory disorder.

It concerns a man who, at the age of forty-five years,
while shovelling snow from the roof of the factory in
which he worked, fell on his head and remained unconscious for half an hour. Then he got up, vomited, climbed

down from the roof, and walked home half a mile. All the time he was suffering from a headache and kept on vomiting and at home he collapsed in a semi-conscious state, but not before giving some account of his accident. In addition to the post-traumatic confusion there were various peripheral neurological signs and a complete incapacity to retain new information. The amnesic disturbance and some peripheral signs, a disordered gait for example, persisted for three years, at which time there was some indication of improvement and also of the patient's desire for recovery. Nevertheless, even at that stage, he would forget his daughter's visit to the hospital when she left the room for a couple of minutes, greet her effusively on her return and express surprise at her knowledge of his accident. Within half an hour, he would also forget having eaten dinner and make excuses for refusing to eat a second meal served to him. Neither recognition nor recall could elicit information imparted in formal learning tests, or indeed of any experience over the past three years, yet the patient's capacity of orientation revealed the retention and use of some recent information. Indeed, he was dimly aware of some gap in his memory, for he felt that the accident had not happened the previous day.

All these anomalies are familiar from amnesic syndromes associated with definite brain lesions, but Syz saw indications of psychogenic factors and these were confirmed by the patient's ability to follow post-hypnotic instructions and by his recollection under hypnosis of certain impressions made during his waking state. Searching for emotional and motivational influences, the desire for financial compensation, a factor common in similar cases, had to be ruled out for this matter had been settled to the patient's satisfaction. Hypnotic and other psychiatric interrogations revealed much, otherwise inaccessible, information concerning the patient's tribulations in marriage. He had married young, chiefly in order to avoid the temptations of promiscuity and alcohol, and thus to satisfy the demands dictated by his moral standards. He

became active in the temperance movement and was noted
for his rigorous sense of justice and morality as well as for
his unusually keen memory. He did well at work and was
happy with his four children, but for many years past
had been sexually frustrated by his wife. Now, while confined to bed after his accident, he overheard a conversation
between his wife and a man in an adjoining room, from
which he concluded that they were engaged in an adulter-
ous relationship.

Whatever the factual basis of the emotional strain
aroused by this suspicion might have been, its significance
for his psychological derangement is attested by the observation that shortly after its revelation, and upon discussions
of the problems it had raised, a marked improvement ensued in the patient's condition. Recovery was
most notable in the peripheral signs, but also extended
to his memory function so that within four months this
reached practically its normal level. Repeated examinations up to fifteen years showed no relapse or serious
disability. Syz interpreted the patient's prolonged neurological and psychiatric disability as a 'means of avoiding a
re-entry into an unbearable life situation'. Although not
severely neurotic prior to the accident, the emotional
shock precipitated by the trauma heightened his propensity to a neurotic response.

While on the face of it, this appears to be a typically
hysterical reaction, Syz argued that it did 'not fit into the
class of hysterical amnesias or fugue states, in which a
circumscribed series of events or perhaps the patient's
own identity is dissociated and forgotten.' The patient's
general disability to recall recent information certainly
distinguished it from the memory disorders attributed to
repression, yet the virtual absence of retrograde amnesia
also marked it off from the amnesic syndrome exemplified,
for example, by Korsakoff's psychosis. Regarding the argument that his patient's disturbance was entirely in recall,
Syz concluded that the retention of some material previously inaccessible to reproduction is no evidence that

'all impressions during the period of disturbed remembering were actually preserved.'

Whether or not Syz's patient had a hysteric personality, there are other examples of patients who developed characteristic hysterical signs, following brain injury, for example paralysis, sensory loss, bizarre postures. Like most patients with hysterical conversion symptoms, these brain-damaged persons are typically poorly educated and poorly endowed for verbal communication. This description does not fit Syz's patient, but it does a more widely debated case, originally reported by Grünthal and Störring (1930a) as 'the first pure case of a man with complete and isolated loss of the registration capacity'.

It concerns a repair mechanic who, at the age of twenty-four years, one day was found unconscious at work as a result of gas poisoning. In the hospital he recovered his health except for a mental disability that restricted his memory span to a maximum of five seconds, disabled him for any new learning and thus also entailed a virtually total disorientation in time, for the surroundings and for persons encountered since the accident. There was no retrogade amnesia except for the circumstances immediately surrounding the accident. The patient's incapacity to resume work was recognized within a few months and he was awarded a 100 per cent compensation. After discharge from the hospital he lived at his parental home but later married and moved with his wife to a different region of Germany.

Systematic observation and experimental tests led the authors to the conclusion that this patient exemplified no derangement in memory function *per se* but only in the registration of information. His perception, judgement and emotional processes were unimpaired, except for situations that depended on the monitoring of the immediately preceding or other recent events. He responded effectively to the normal biological signals and readily complied with instructions imposed by others but was unable to carry them out past the initial moves. No evi-

dence of residual or latent learning effects could be detected, not even of repeated painful pin pricks, except in
the patient's autonomic function which eventually also
prompted him to flight.

The authors confirmed their initial findings in a follow-
up study three years later (Grünthal and Störring, 1930b),
but further examinations by other investigators after
another two decades indicated some important changes in
this patient's psychopathology, although for all practical
purposes his incapacity to retain new information remained as complete as ever. A lively, and at times acri-
monious, polemic ensued between the defenders of the
original report and their critics who diagnosed hysteria. In
the face of the observations reported by their supporters
as well as their critics, Grünthal and Störring (1956) revised their position, concluding that over the years the
effects of poisoning had been superseded by symptoms
attributable to hysteria and malingering. The part played
by malingering in patients of this type is difficult to determine, especially as the boundary between deliberate faking
and unconscious motivation is not sharply discernible.

Motivated Distortions of Memory

Repression is only one of the manifestations of motivational effects on memory and learning. Closely related to
it is the mechanism of denial, and influences originating
from the same sources are capable of radically distorting
memories by condensation, displacement and other mechanisms described by Freud and his school that also parallel several attitudinal determinants of remembering listed
by Bartlett and his followers. Most of these mechanisms
become particularly accentuated in patients who are subject to delusions, either chronically or transiently in fever,
under the effect of alcohol or of other toxic agents.

The psychoneuroses other than hysteria are not noted
for specific disorders of memory or learning, except for
the inability in learning how to cope with situations so as

to overcome a disabling symptom. Phobic patients cannot learn, without appropriate thereapeutic help, to enter situations that frighten them. Anxious patients cannot learn to ignore their objectively unfounded fears. Compulsive persons cannot learn to desist from their irrational rituals. Apart from these disabilities in learning, however, they do not display characteristic memory disorders.

Depressive patients, however – especially the psychotic – are both impaired in their capacity for new learning and have a propensity to distort the content of their memories in recall. The former disability stems from lack of concentration, the latter from a pervasive sense of guilt and self-deprecation which infuses quite innocent episodes of the personal past with imaginary transgressions. While the misconstruction of memories in accordance with such morbid ethical judgements is quite common in depressed patients, it is not unknown in relatively healthy persons, especially while they are in psychiatric treatment and mull over their past with unusual preoccupation. An example in point is that of a man who recalled, with a considerable sense of guilt, a childhood episode that had involved an elder brother as well as a baby brother in a pram. The man remembered being in charge of the pram and then letting it roll down a slope, so that it hit a lamp post, turned over and the baby was thrown on to the pavement. Fortunately no serious harm had befallen the infant, but many years afterwards the man was still worried that his apparent irresponsibility at the time of the incident might have been motivated by a hidden desire to hurt his baby brother. Later he discovered from his elder brother that, on the occasion of that harmless accident, the elder brother was pushing the pram and responsible for letting it roll down the pavement.

Although the mental disorders associated with schizophrenia are primarily disturbances in the thought processes, they have in numerous instances been traced to emotional and motivational sources. Regarding amnesic derangements in schizophrenia Ey (1950), for example, has made a strong case for emotional determinants, citing the case of two young patients who had completely forgotten their marriages. The argument rests in still stronger foundations when it concerns the paranoid type of schizophrenic.

Most schizophrenic patients are extremely poor learners because of their deficient attention. Their inordinate susceptibility to distraction impairs the operations necessary for recall as well as the organizing processes in registration. The sudden intrusion of ideas from objectively unrelated contexts, and errors of judgement that extend even to the recognition of their personal identity, produce anomalies that are apt to occur in the schizophrenic patient's memories as well as in his immediate evaluation of a situation.

Self-accusatory delusions, similar to those of the patient who falsely remembered his part in a slight accident of a baby brother, are quite typical of schizophrenic patients, but are based, not on actual events which they had witnessed, but on mere imagination. An example in point is the young woman who recollects from her past an attempt to throw her baby sister out of the window, in which she was prevented only by her mother's timely arrival. In fact, at the time of this imaginary episode, the older sister was barely three years old and quite unable to lift the baby up to the window. She was, however, big enough to nurture murderous thoughts towards her. Such errors in recollection are quite likely to arise from a confusion of fact with fantasy.

Unlike the distorted memories of the depressed, those of schizophrenic patients are by no means always self-accusatory. It is not uncommon for them to attack another patient or a ward orderly in a fit of violence and then to recall the incident as if they had been attacked by the other person. This kind of distortion in memory would be quite typical of the paranoid schizophrenic whose misconstructions in perception, reasoning and recall are all determined by motivational factors.

Paranoid persons often function quite successfully in society but, like those whose psychosis necessitates retraint in a mental hospital, misconstrue observed events and intentions inferred in other people, so as to fit their extremely comprehensive delusional system which is typically raised upon the suspicion of some widely organized persecution directed against themselves. Their memories are as apt to be misconstrued in accordance with their delusions, as are their perceptions and thought processes, and they are most resistant to learning that conflicts with their rigidly preconceived notions. While palpably inaccurate in many respects, the content of recall, far from undergoing any diminution, is quite apt to be excessively detailed. This propensity, classified as hypermnesia in the clinical literature and characteristic of the paranoid type, has also been reported of other schizophrenic patients.

6 Impaired Capacity of Learning and Memory

Learning and memory disorders generated or sustained by unconscious motives or by more or less deliberate malingering can revert to completely normal function. Recovery is, of course, the more likely if the disturbance is not associated with permanent damage to brain tissue. Remission implies that the order stemmed from an impediment in the application of an ability which itself has remained unimpaired. Such examples of amnesia are not all of the psychogenic type. They can be observed in patients who have lost consciousness as a result of a toxic or infectious attack on the central nervous system, of a physical as well as of an emotional shock.

The amnesic derangement can be of very brief duration as in the examples described by Fisher and Adams (1964), for example, in which there is no loss of consciousness, or it can extend but a short distance either way from the period covered by impaired consciousness. Epileptic seizures furnish the most fully described example of transient amnesias and also of a mental disturbance associated with a derangement in the electrophysiological function of the brain. Several of the severe amnesic disorders can be attributed to clearly localized lesions in the brain, others appear to be caused by more diffuse damage to cerebral tissue. In still other instances abnormal biochemical or metabolic function may be the source of the mental disturbance. The latter explanation has been validated in certain types of mental deficiency.

Mental deficiency

In mental deficiency, an extremely low capacity for new learning constitutes the core of the general intellectual impairment and reflects a failure to process and organize information. Experiments with very simple tasks show that, having reached the same level of initial learning, the mental defectives retain the material as effectively as matched control subjects. Indeed, there have been reports on memory prodigies who, for example, displayed a seemingly unlimited capacity to remember names or dates, yet had to be diagnosed as feeble-minded.

Epilepsy

The controversies that surround the problem of epilepsy do not centre on the memory disorder associated with this electrophysiological disturbance. Whether the fits involve motor symptoms or not, whether they can be traced to a focal lesion in the brain or, for the lack of other evidence, must be attributed to biochemical or psychogenic sources, they interrupt the patient's normal state of consciousness. During the seizure he may have hallucinations or automatisms, that is, carry out actions that in certain instances are entirely appropriate to the situation – continue driving a car, for example – but subsequently will have no recollection of them. In this respect automatisms resemble fugue states (cf. p. 99), and other parallels between epileptic and hysteric symptoms have also been remarked on. Very rarely a patient is able to recall later some of his actions or observations during a fit, and sometimes they re-emerge in the indefinite character of dream memories.

The amnesic disturbance in epilepsy is not limited to the incidents that occur during the seizure. It usually extends to events that preceded the fit by at least a few seconds, and sometimes by several minutes or even hours, that is, to events that the patient has observed quite clearly and in which he may have played an active and intelligent part. The memory of these events may be recovered, typically by stages and in the reverse order to their proximity to the seizure. This component of the memory disturbance is customarily referred to as *retrograde amnesia*, but there is good reason to follow Burnham (1904) (cf. p. 57) in distinguishing amnesias limited to spans of a few seconds, minutes, or hours as *retroactive* from those that effectively delete memories of several years and, on occasion, of the patient's entire adult life.

The memory disorder also extends forward to events in which the epileptic patient may seem to function quite normally. This *post-ictal* amnesia is of brief duration unless several seizures follow in quick succession and may be manifested only by an extraordinary susceptibility to distraction, but its effects do not shrink with time as do the retroactive amnesias. The latter, especially the retroactive amnesias observed in cases of concussion, have been extensively quoted in support of the consolidation theory and the evidence was cited in that connexion further back (p. 57). Epileptic amnesias also furnish compelling arguments for distinguishing the brain mechanisms that subserve immediate registration from those involved in the subsequent fixation of new information. Whereas epileptic patients typically recall nothing that took place during a seizure, experiments to impart new learning to them while in a twilight state have shown savings in subsequent tests of relearning. The observation that intense concentration helps to shorten the period of retroactive amnesia suggests that consolidation, that is, the process with which the abnormal electrophysiological activity interferes, is not of an all-or-none character. Apparently information can be filed either in stable systems with multiple access or only tenuously and with fewer avenues of approach.

Temporal and Frontal Lobectomies

Most remarkable for the student of memory disorders are the epilepsies originating in the temporal lobes. One of their characteristic symptoms is a derangement in the sense of familiarity. They produce both the loss of familiarity manifest in depersonalization and the type of false recognition best known under the description of *déjà vu*. Depersonalization, as distinct from the loss of personal identity, entails feelings of unreality regarding oneself, one's body or the external world. *Déjà vu*, discussed more fully in the next chapter, is the experience of having seen before something or somebody who in fact is being encountered for the first time.

Patients with epileptic foci in the temporal lobe have been helped by surgical removal of the diseased brain tissue. Wilder Penfield of Montreal was one of the pioneers of this operative technique and he investigated his patients with a view to the light their disturbances might throw on the cerebral mechanisms involved in remembering. In the course of such research, Penfield (Penfield and Jasper, 1954) experimented with electric stimulation of the temporal lobes exposed for surgery. He noted in several patients that if the electrodes were in contact with the lateral, and more frequently still with the superior surface of either the healthy or diseased temporal lobe, stimulation elicited some personal memory. This could be an emotionally charged episode, a song, the face or voice of a friend or an unidentified voice heard as if it came over the radio. Stimulation of the same spot evoked the same memory or hallucinatory image and its associated ideas and affect. Furthermore, if experienced as a memory, it was the memory of a specific occasion, whereas in normal remembering we usually recall a song apart from the circumstances that attended its hearing, a friend as a composite image rather than the way he appeared or sounded on a particular occasion. These artificially evoked auditory and visual images were often reported to be like dream memories, differing from normal memories in their vividness, contextual setting and other qualities. They can, nevertheless, be cited as yet another observation in abnormal psychology to support the tenet that human memory preserves past experiences in discrete units as well as in composite forms or schemata.

Amnesic disturbance

Although one must exercise caution in generalizing to normal function from observations made on diseased brains, it seems that the temporal lobes offer an access to the memory files and are therefore likely to be involved in the operations of both purposeful and involuntary recall. At the same time, the transient amnesias consequent upon temporal lobe seizures suggest that disturbances in the neuroelectric function of this brain area interfere with the operations necessary for the registration of new information. The memory disturbance may become permanent after temporal lobectomy but only if the hippocampus is excized and if both lobes are affected. The case for an amnesic disorder following unilateral temporal lobectomy has been controversial. Penfield and Brenda Milner (1958), his associate in much of this research, believe that removal of one temporal lobe results in chronic memory defects only if the other temporal lobe has been diseased, for example, through a birth injury. Otherwise, unilateral temporal lobectomy only perpetuates some pre-existing and relatively mild disabilities: difficulties in verbal or, according to Meyer (1959), in auditory learning, if the dominant (typically left) hemisphere is resected, defects in the recognition of visual patterns and of melodies (but not of pitch or rhythm) if the operation was on the non-dominant side.

The few patients who have developed severe memory disturbances after temporal lobe lesions, both as a result of surgery or from natural causes, present a picture similar to that which has been studied more extensively and manifested more severely in the amnesic syndrome. Even though they may continue with their work and exercise their well established skills, they run into difficulties in carrying out instructions, in dealing with administrative details, that is, with executing the successive steps of an action plan. Their performance in tests of immediate recall is quite efficient but they cannot learn material that has to be encoded for registration. They rapidly forget even those tests which they perform successfully and may not recognize their own drawings after a few minutes' delay. Retrogade amnesia is not uncommon, although the temporal span affected is usually quite modest in comparison with, for example, the Korsakoff syndrome; and there are also reports of inactivity, of much reduced initiative associated with the amnesic defects. These derangements become chronic and can be observed long after the remission of the confusional, dysphasic and other immediately post-operative signs. Blakemore and Falconer (1967), however, have found that the auditory learning deficit disappears with the passage of years.

Frontal lobes

Removal or destruction by disease of other cortical areas does not produce specific memory or learning defects. Diffuse damage is likely to impair old established aptitudes as well as new learning, and such performances testing attention as the memory span. The short-term effects of major brain surgery include several signs of memory and learning deficit, disorders in orientation, an abnormal susceptibility to distraction, a lack of initiative, and a propensity to confuse fact with fantasy or to misplace true memories in their chronological setting. These disorders have been described most fully in connexion with frontal lobotomies, that is, in patients who had been severely disturbed prior to their operation. Follow-up studies furnish no conclusive evidence for any permanent memory or learning deficit as a result of frontal lobectomy, although some of the patients studied by Kral and Durost (1953) had difficulties in retaining new experiences for as long as two or three years after the operation.

There is reason to believe that the frontal lobes play an important part in early learning but less so in adulthood, although Barbizet (1965) regards their intact function necessary for the acquisition of complex concepts and also for the recall of those that were registered before the brain lesion. In so far as psychotic patients benefit from the ablation or functional severance of their frontal lobes, their capacity for learning and remembering is likely to increase. Lesions in this area of the cortex may have more

deleterious effects on patients who were not previously in-
capacitated by chronic mental illness. While a study of a
group of men with penetrating frontal lobe wounds
showed no specific memory defect, I have observed two
men who had developed a fully fledged amnesic syndrome
following a successful operation by Drs Sweet and Ballantine for an aneurysm of the anterior communicating
artery (Talland, Sweet and Ballantine, 1967). Although
there is no reason to believe that their brain damage
affected the temporal lobes or the limbic system, their
memory disturbance was barely distinguishable from that
associated with lesions in those areas and their learning
impairment extended to quite simple tasks.

Traumatic Amnesias

Two of the major causes of traumatic amnesias are concussions and wounds inflicted by 'small metal fragments
travelling at high velocity'. Russell (1959), whose definition is quoted here and who has studied traumatic amnesias over several decades, distinguishes two types of
missile wounds: those that penetrate the skull and others
that glance away from the skull but by their impact may
force bone fragments to some depth into the brain. Regarding closed head injuries, Russell traces the most disas-
trous examples to road accidents with high-powered
motor cycles; with increased affluence, of course, automo-
biles figure more prominently in the case records.

Post-traumatic amnesia

Penetrating brain wounds can have quite devastating effects
on mental function. If the damage is confined to the left
temporal lobe, however, the principal defect is the patient's
inability to remember current events. He may also show
signs of limited retroactive and post-traumatic amnesias
but is likely to recall the circumstances of his injury. Severe
concussions, unlike many penetrating wounds, cause loss of
consciousness and the victim cannot remember the details

of the accident. Such accidents, too, can cause total dementia but often enough the damage is reversible, especially in
younger patients. In most of the cases (for example in 890
out of a series of 1,029 analysed by Russell) the amnesia
includes a retroactive component which in the majority of
the patients extended over less than thirty minutes and
typically only over a few seconds.

Another facet of the mental derangement associated
with head injuries is the post-traumatic amnesia, that is,
the patient's inability to remember events experienced for
some time after his recovery of consciousness. The duration of the post-traumatic amnesia tends to be propor-
tionate to the extent of the retroactive amnesia, but is
typically longer, with a modal length of between one and
twenty-four hours in Russell's sample of 1,029 cases. This
disturbance may continue for a while after the patient
appears to be fully aware of his surrounding. Boxers and
football players, for example, often continue the fight or
game after concussion, yet have no recollection later of
anything they had done during that period.

Retroactive amnesia

In the early stages of traumatic amnesia the patient may
appear much like those suffering from delirium and talk
as cheerfully as well as senselessly as is common in alcoholic intoxication. He is apt to be confused, especially
about the circumstances of his accident, and may substitute for it a true accident that he suffered some years
earlier or reconstruct it in part from the actual details but
so that it fits his delusional scheme. Russell reported an
example in which a patient who had been thrown from his
motor cycle as he was swerving to avoid a dog later
accused the dog's owner as well as the animal of having
attacked him. He was determined to drag the imaginary
assailant to court and had the satisfaction of believing
that the dog's owner had already been arrested on the
patient's charge. In fact, his only contact with the dog's
owner took place when the latter accompanied him in the

ambulance from the site of the accident to the hospital.

The case is reminiscent of Dr Somerville's experience with another, non-motorized, cyclist, quoted in chapter 1. There are any number of examples of post-traumatic amnesia in the medical literature but as a remarkable parallel to Somerville's other case, let us admit an illustration from fiction. In *Among the Cinders*, Maurice Shadbolt (1965) describes a hunting trip in the mountains of New Zealand undertaken by two youngsters, Sam, a Maori, and Nick, a white boy whom Sam's family had virtually adopted. After various adventures the last day comes with no game in sight, then some animal moves in the bush, Nick aims and shoots a wild goat. Nick is disgusted with himself for killing a beast that offers neither food nor sport and as the wounded goat plunges over the edge of the hill, he blames himself for putting an end to a life that was harmless, happy and had a better right to the hill than himself. Then he stumbles on a cave that on closer inspection turns out to be a Maori burial ground and, largely in order to get his own back over a slight, Nick calls Sam and tells him to look into the cave. The Maori boy is terrified at what he finds there and in his panicky escape tumbles over a precipice. Nick, alarmed, climbs after him and reaches the bottom, sorely bruised, with broken bones, and concussed. He takes the dying Sam in his arms and there they stay until a rescue party finds them four days later, one boy unconscious and the other dead. Nick gradually recovers in the hospital, learns of Sam's fate and insists on confessing to the constable that he had shot his friend before his fall. The thoughts, he believes, that accompanied his crime are the same sentiments that plagued him after killing the goat, after he had in fact fired his last shot – for no bullet wound could be found in Sam's body.

The fictitious example condenses two episodes so as to provide evidence for the innocent victim of concussion to blame himself. There may be similar instances in the clinical literature but the typical case is the reverse, in which the victim accuses an innocent bystander of hurting him. He may not persist for long with the false charges, although he is unlikely to regain an accurate picture of the circumstances of the accident, even as the retroactive amnesia diminishes. This happens quite regularly, partly with the help of informants who remind the patient of incidents he has forgotten, partly with the help of fortuitous reminders, but largely as a spontaneous process, although the process can be speeded up by the patient's own efforts.

Recovery from retroactive amnesia may take longer than recovery from post-traumatic amnesia. Russell, in agreement with most students of traumatic amnesias, stresses the orderly shrinkage of the retroactive amnesia. The most distant memories are the first to return, then more recent ones, until only the events of the last few days or perhaps the last few minutes preceding the accident are still unavailable for recall. Zangwill and Whitty (1966) dispute the strict chronological order of recovery, and propose that this proceeds around 'islands of memory' that emerge in quite haphazard order. In the more severe cases the recovery is never complete and just as the process starts with the recovery of 'islands of memory', it terminates with 'islands of amnesia' still left in the midst of an otherwise coherent record of the patient's past. Both interpretations are in agreement that emotionally significant or otherwise important events are neither necessarily the first nor the most certain to be remembered. Some of the details of the accident – an experience that was undoubtedly emotionally charged – may emerge later in the form of hallucinatory visions, although never in voluntary recall. Like certain observations made during epileptic seizures, these details seem to have been registered at a level that is beyond the reach of normal recollection.

Post-E.C.T. amnesia

A third type of traumatic amnesia is that associated with electroconvulsive shock treatment (E.C.T.) administered

to psychotic patients and at times to relieve otherwise intractable pain. The manner in which E.C.T. exerts a
therapeutic effect is unknown, but must be consequent
upon the violent upheaval it causes in the neuroelectrical
function of the brain. Understandably enough, the
patient registers experiences during shock no better than
in an epileptic fit; a brief retroactive amnesia is also
characteristic of E.C.T. The effect this type of shock
exerts on memory is difficult to evaluate nowadays, since
patients are usually anaesthetized prior to treatment and
recover their consciousness some time after its termination. In past days, when anaesthesia was not a standard
procedure, patients often showed intense fear and panicky
resistance when lined up for repeated E.C.T., thus indicating some memory of previous treatments or at least
of their affective quality. For different reasons, it is almost
impossible to assess the long-term effects of a series of
shock treatments on memory and learning capacity, since
patients selected for this type of therapy are so disturbed
to begin with as to function well below their normal levels.

A few observational and experimental studies offer some
data about the effects of E.C.T. on memory. The retroactive amnesia extends over a few seconds and, according
to Cronholm and Ottoson (1963), tends to decrease with
ultra-brief stimuli. Sometimes, as Williams (1950) noted,
patients recall information imparted to them just before
or just after E.C.T. as if it had been a dream experience.
Cronholm and his associates demonstrated decrements in
learning, retention and recall six hours (Cronholm and
Mollander, 1957) and a week (Cronholm and Blomquist,
1959) after E.C.T. but none after a month (Cronholm and
Mollander, 1964).

The post-traumatic amnesia following E.C.T. is most
conspicuous in its effect on new learning, which far out-
weighs the retroactive amnesia. Williams demonstrated
experimentally that recognition after E.C.T. is facilitated
by previous exposure to the test material, even though the
patient has no recollection of seeing it before. In one of

our studies, patients presented with narrative passages for first learning before and for relearning after E.C.T., tended to repeat errors they had made on the first occasion but often remembered neither having been tested on the same text previously, nor indeed having already had E.C.T. Prompting can quite markedly improve performance at this stage, suggesting that much that appears to be a deficit in learning and retention may be primarily a defect in recall.

While the immediate amnesic effects of E.C.T. are indisputable, there is no conclusive evidence from controlled studies that a long series of E.C.T. damages memory or learning notably, although this has been the impression of many clinical observers. The long term effects, of course, depend on the efficacy of treatment and possibly also on the personality structure of the patient. For example Stengel (1950) has argued that E.C.T. can elicit a hysterical amnesia as well as do other traumatic incidents.

The Amnesic Syndrome

The amnesias produced by brain traumas are characteristically of short duration, and the retroactive component may be entirely absent or tends to recede in the course of recovery. In other instances of severe memory disturbance, the retrograde and anterograde amnesias are closely associated and extensive. They are invariably so in those chronic mental disorders that are classified under the head of the amnesic syndrome.

In the amnesic syndrome the memory defects constitute the most prominent, although not the only, abnormality. The mental disturbance Milner (1965) has described as characteristic of bilateral temporal lobectomy belongs within this syndrome, as do the chronic memory disorders associated with lesions or tumours in the limbic system, with toxemias or infections attacking the region of the third ventricle and with prolonged anoxia which causes permanent brain damage. The most commonly observed and most exhaustively studied example of the amnesic syndrome is Korsakoff's psychosis, a disease typically attributed to alcoholism and to a concomitant nutritional deficiency. Korsakoff's psychosis presents an irreversible and virtually stable mental derangement. It may also, like amnesic syndromes of other origins, follow a course of gradual deterioration into a state of dementia. Examples of progressive, albeit partial, recovery are rare if the disease has reached the chronic stage. In some patients the amnesic syndrome constitutes the initial phase of the disease and terminates abruptly in delirium, coma and death. It can, however, also be of limited duration, for example, when associated with states of clouded consciousness as a result of infection or poisoning or with a cyst in the region of the third ventricle which in due course empties spontaneously.

In their initial phase most examples of the amnesic syndrome are marked by a confusional state so complete that the patient appears to be demented. He is apt to be delusional, apathetic or agitated and out of touch with his surroundings. His conversation, if coherent at all, is studded with those inaccuracies and improbabilities that are described as confabulation. His memory for recent experiences and – as far as can be ascertained – for those that pre-dated his illness is strikingly depleted but this anomaly gains prominence only as, in the course of recovery, the other manifestations of mental disturbance recede along with the peripheral neuropathy that is characteristic of the early phase in the alcoholic Korsakoff syndrome.

Anterograde amnesia

Past the acute stage of disturbance, the amnesic patient is capable of paying attention to his environment and of engaging in rational conversation but is still likely to show signs of gross disorientation. He rarely grasps the situation in which he is placed, is apt to mistake the hospital for some other place he used to know before his illness and to cast doctors, nurses and visitors into roles that fit that familiar setting. He is also disoriented in time, unaware of the weeks or months that have elapsed since his initial breakdown. Indeed, even after many years of hospitalization, the patient thinks of himself, of his wife and children as if they were the same age as they had reached at the beginning of his illness. He may know the date, the year, perhaps the month and day of the month as well and by subtracting the date of his birth arrive at his correct age, and then reconstruct the actual ages of others, but there remains a wide gap between the result of this arithmetic exercise and what he feels. A sexagernarian patient I studied was quite capable of figuring out that his children were no longer in their teens but that is how he thought he had seen them only a few weeks earlier. Another patient always believed that she had been brought to the hospital the day before, and did so with as much apparent conviction eight years after her admission as she had done when her hospitalization could still be viewed as transitional (Talland, 1965).

If time has come to a stop for the amnesic patient, it is because he remembers virtually none of the events that he has witnessed since the onset of his illness. The days go by and none seems to be different from the others. Staff members and fellow patients re-appear looking no more familiar than complete strangers. A story gives as much satisfaction on tenth as it did on first reading, its novelty never seems to wear off. If the patient recognizes a new figure in his environment, his doctor for example, as some one familiar, he may still easily confuse him with another figure encountered in the same environment or name him correctly but as diffidently as if it were a wild guess. In the literature there are several accounts of the medical examination that had to be interrupted for a few minutes, in which the patient greeted the doctor on his return as some one he had not met for a long time.

Learning deficit

As they keep but the spottiest record of their everyday experiences, so amnesic patients are virtually incapable of accomplishing any formal learning. Several authors have stated that the anterograde amnesia – the patient's failure to retain new information – is more disabling with regard to personal experiences than to the impersonal material presented in experiments of learning and memory, yet nothing could be forgotten more rapidly or totally than is the content of laboratory tasks by amnesic patients. Figure 4 illustrates the rate at which a group of 16 Korsakoff patients forgot in repeated tests of free recall the few items initially learnt in three minutes from a list of ten monosyllabic words. It also shows their mean incorrect responses and comparable data obtained from a control group of sixteen alcohol addicts matched for age, who had no severe memory disturbance. It is evident that the amnesic patients learned considerably less of this material than the control subjects and more striking still was the steeper rate at which they lost the information held in immediate recall. For those who are impressed with these patients' frequent inability to retain a name, an address, or any other item of information even for a couple of minutes, the significant aspect of the graph is that the patients' recall scores remained well above zero over a span of twelve minutes.

Indeed, amnesic patients – except those who are too disturbed to grasp the instruction – typically perform within normal limits in tests of immediate recall, such as the standard digit span. They are also likely to retain this type of material for a while, if uninterrupted by other activity, but forget rapidly and irreversibly if their attention is deflected from the task at some point between registration and recall, or when the encoding processes entailed in registration themselves create interference. This happens in most life situations that would provide material for remembering, as it does in many learning tasks. It did not happen in my repeated recall test of ten-word lists, for the subjects were not busy with other tasks between the probes, nor did they engage in conversation and, unlike most normal people, may indeed have sat

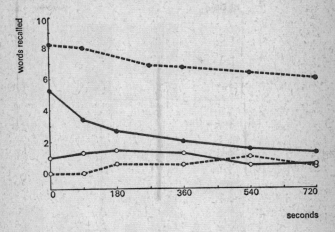

●   correct
○   incorrect
———   Korsakoff
- - - - -   control

Figure 4 Repeated recall of C-V-C words by sixteen Korsakoff patients and sixteen control subjects

there with their minds blank and unperturbed by an extraneous thought.

The effect of interference on short-term retention is quite apparent from the histogram in Figure 5. This summarizes the performance of the same two groups of sixteen in four tests of recall of a ten-word sentence immediately after vocal presentation and five minutes later. Four sentences, matched in difficulty, were learned at intervals of a week, each time with a different activity between immediate and delayed recall. These consisted of a manual task, a learning test, an interview probing some emotionally neutral childhood memories, and of no structured activity at all. Tested immediately after presentation, the two groups recalled the sentences equally well; in delayed recall the control group always surpassed the

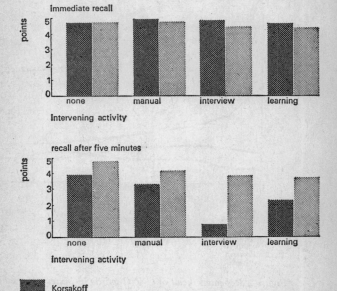

Figure 5 Immediate and delayed recall of a ten-word sentence with different intervening activities by sixteen Korsakoff patients and sixteen control subjects

Korsakoff patients and the margin of their superiority increased with the interference of the interpolated activity. This was strongest as a result of the interview which fully engaged the patients' attention and most completely deflected their orientation from the test sentence. It was less so with the intervening second learning task which most of them attempted with the barest involvement and pursued with little success.

My experiments with amnesic patients have furnished several instances of their failure to resume activities interrupted by alternative tasks and there is ample evidence from other investigators of their extraordinary distractibility. These patients cannot pick up the thread after dropping it for the merest moment and this defect seems closely related to their inability to structure temporally sequential impressions into unitary experiences. This inability has been demonstrated experimentally in the patients' perceptual function, in studies that presented them with meaningful texts for comprehension and learning, and is also apparent in the manner in which they go through life, existing – as some observers have remarked – in cross-sections, without any temporal continuity.

Life experienced without temporal continuity must be like the fragmentary contents of dreams and indeed several writers have compared the memories of amnesic patients with dream memories. Further evidence for the dreamlike quality of their memories is based on the diffidence that is so characteristic of these patients' rare achievements in recalling incidents that have occurred during their stay in the hospital and in the recognition of people they have met there. Such successes in remembering seem to be entirely unrelated to the emotional impact or personal significance of the original event. Examples of new learning are rare and most likely to be observed in the acquisition of a new motor skill, although many amnesic patients do also learn some new names, the address of their hospital and their way about there, the places where various things are kept.

Several of the pioneer students of the Korsakoff syndrome noted that at some later date patients behaved as if they remembered incidents of which they appeared to be quite oblivious at the time of their occurrence. They also demonstrated savings in formal learning tests and from these observations the authors were tempted to conclude that considerable latent learning had taken place under the surface of an apparently total anterograde amnesia. Many other investigators, however, have been unsuccessful in attempts to find indications of latent learning, with or without the aid of hypnosis. Their failure may weaken the case for, but does not refute, the argument that in the amnesic syndrome the basic derangement is in recall and that the patient's registration and retention are no more seriously impaired than his perception or reasoning, functions that are substantially undamaged in this disease.

Retrograde amnesia

On the face of it, anterograde amnesia is a disturbance in registration or retention, or both. The patient's capacity to recall is never so severely damaged as to account for his inability to remember virtually nothing of what he perceives and moreover his learning deficit is hardly relieved if tested by recognition rather than by recall of reproduction. Yet, along with the anterograde deficit there is always a considerable gap in the recollection of the patient's pre-morbid history. Korsakoff patients labour under the handicap of a retrograde amnesia that extends in time far beyond the episodes of their breakdown and the immediately preceding events. Cases have been known in which all the decades of adult life seem to have vanished without a trace in memory and it is not uncommon for patients to be unaware of ever having married or having borne and raised children, even though their lives in the family spanned several decades. In most instances the retrograde amnesia is not quite so global, but many important as well as the less significant experiences are inaccessible to recall or are available in fragments isolated from their context.

Memories of the past do not usually remain in complete isolation, more typically they are recollected in an incorrect temporal context and situational setting – for example, an accident suffered in one job as if it had happened in another job, a true encounter with a person at a date when the latter was dead – and thus the patient gets involved in contradictions that are apparent to the observer but not to him. Freed from the constraint of temporal continuity, at one moment he fancies himself as he was just after leaving school and falsely states his age as sixteen; then, in reply to a question about his children, he easily slides into the immediate past and correctly reports that he has four, all grown up by now. These contradictions, these misplacements of true events in their chronological setting, provide the material of confabulations rather than do imaginative fabrications, deliberate lies or even desperate attempts to fill in memory gaps.

Retrograde amnesia is not confined to personal experiences. Amnesic patients typically have but the haziest recollections of public events and tend to confuse the setting and chronological order of those they remember. Obviously enough, they take little note of political events and changes that happen during their illness but very often they name as the present head of the state a monarch or president whose reign or tenure terminated long before the onset of their amnesic disorder. While the records of so many once-solidly registered experiences are unavailable to the patients and hardly any new such records are accumulated during their illness, their command of well-practised skills remains undiminished. These include spoken and written language, the elementary rules of social intercourse, as well as the special skills of a trade and even the application of such elaborate sets of rules as a game of chess or the solution of mathematical problems demand. There are reports of amnesic patients learning new skills or playing unfamiliar music on the piano, but after a short while they remember having played the piano no better than the psychological laboratory tasks which they may have performed quite successfully.

Disorder of mood and sustained action

Amnesic patients have no clear insight into the severity of their mental disturbance. Many seem as if they had no inkling at all that they are impaired, others vaguely realize that something is amiss but not the full extent of their deficit. A gradual comprehension of their condition takes place as they pass from the acute confusional to the chronic amnesic state; and those who recover from the latter, for example tuberculous meningitis cases described by Williams and Smith (1954), can attain to perfect insight even while left with a comparatively severe retrograde amnesia.

The depressive appearance of so many amnesic patients in the chronic phase of their illness is therefore not directly attributable to despair over their condition and future prospects. It reflects rather an emptiness of interest and lack of spontaneity that is as characteristic of the syndrome as the memory defects. Not only in psychological tests do these patients fail to show the least initiative, they do so in social situations as well, seeking none but routine occupations nor the company of special friends. The carefree mood characteristic of the early stages of their illness gradually gives way to one of detachment; outward signs of emotion are few and of momentary duration if they do occur. These patients are as incapable of sustaining an affective response as they are of sustaining the operations that are necessary to file information for future reference, or those required for the retrieval of information in recall.

Experiences, items of impersonal information that are but tenuously registered, are difficult to recall later at will, but there is always some chance of recovering them. This accounts for the odd occasions when amnesic patients do succeed in recall. Since their capacity to complete the operations necessary for recall is also severely impaired, the chances of such successes are slight, but they do increase if the patient makes a recovery. Recognition should be more successful but is not notably so, because amnesic patients also fail in those operations of testing and checking for fit that precede correct recognition. It has been argued that these patients display an abnormal deficiency of the critical attitude. They do so because the appreciation and correction of errors in memory demands the ability to compare the image or message produced with a model that is not within sensory reach, a flexibility in alternating sets that amnesic patients cannot master. Furthermore, they also miss those contextual cues that help to correct incipient errors in normal recognition and recall.

Amnesia refers to the total unavailability of memories, to complete failure in learning, and there is abundant evidence of both in the patients under review, but this evidence should not obscure the fact that both the anterograde and retrograde variety is also riddled with instances of paramnesias – of partially correct, or misplaced and jumbled memories.

Memory and Old Age

Normal ageing

Anecdotal evidence, introspective reports, casual observations all indicate that the capacity to acquire new information and to recall at will at least recent memories declines with the advancing years. This process of deterioration is clearly not co-extensive with maturation or indeed with ageing past maturity. Typically, it becomes apparent in the seventh decade and then more widespread as well as steeper with advancing age, but there is much interpersonal variability in this respect, so that many septuagenarians have resisted the ravages of ageing with remarkable success. This variability within a uniform trend shows that what we regard as the normal process of ageing is a compound of a progressive trend of decomposition and disorganization in the biological systems of the body and of discrete accidents that hit these systems randomly and with cumulative effects.

As in the amnesic syndrome, no one constituent process of learning and remembering is exclusively susceptible to the deleterious effects of ageing, but registration appears to be relatively more affected than recall or recognition.

Old people fall farther below the standards set by the young in tasks that demand new learning, the reproduction or recognition of recently registered information, than in performance that depends on the exercise of old established skills or memory for relatively distant events. Several reasons have been given for this age-related deficit, including reduced motivation, a negative attitude to novelty, a reduced general state of arousal or its opposite, heightened arousal, with a consequent enhancement of interference from the autonomic system.

The evidence for a reduced capacity to process incoming information with advancing age is quite strong, but the belief that old memories are retained intact while new ones are rapidly lost does not rest on equally solid foundations. This widely held view has been disputed by a number of investigators and some others who endorse it ascribe the differential effect to repeated subliminal rehearsals of the early records. Another consideration in support of this view is that the categories according to which information is filed for storage were established by early learning, by temporally distant experiences. Most subsequent learning or registration had to fit into some such category as well as it could, but certainly no more closely than the data that served as its model. Moreover, to the extent that new information did not fit into a pre-established category, the latter had to be modified or unlearnt. Much recent learning can be achieved only at the cost of some unlearning and the longer one lives the more likely it is that one must pay this price. The demand to guard a record from assimilation or distortion increases with age but so also does the effort to meet any such demand, for the capacity to process incoming information shrinks with the advancing years.

There are probably several reasons for this contraction in capacity, all related to changes in the central nervous system and other physiological systems of the organism. Speed is almost certainly one of the factors or the rate at which the incoming data can be ordered and transformed into codable records. Susceptibility to interference effects inherent in the operations of registration and recall also increases with age and consequently more information tends to be lost in the course of both processes. The data available for filing are more fragmentary and thus less suitable for efficient coding, while those extracted from the files are apt to be incomplete. Reduced activity rate and a heightened vulnerability to interference also impair the search operations in recall, so that these may entirely fail of their objective. Errors in recall by incorrect substitution are comparatively few in old age. The capacity to test the accuracy or appropriateness of data seems to be unimpaired except for a tendency to perseveration or stereotypy. Temporal misplacements of true memories obviously also increase with the advancing years.

Senile and pre-senile dementias

A willingness to use interchangeably such terms as senility and senescence, and perhaps also ageing, may but reflect a cavalier use of technical terms, but it can as well express the view that the psychoses of the senium represent a more advanced stage of the mental deterioration that – sooner or later – is generally discernible in the normal process of ageing. The argument for this opinion is a flimsy one based on the observation that the defects characteristic of normal ageing and of senility show some common features and that which is common to both differs in degree. To be sure, the memory and learning deficit of the normal septuagenarian is present in the senile psychoses, but constitutes only a part within a larger pattern and the pattern itself is a variable one.

Senility is a collective term that refers to several nosologically distinct mental disturbances. These include the psychoses and other brain diseases observed in the young as well as in the old, which, however, may hit the latter with more destructive effect because of their lower resistance, especially in the vascular system. Senility often denotes an amnesic syndrome that starts and develops in old age, and is in all essentials identical with other examples of this mental disease. In order to distinguish it from other similar psychoses it has been called *presbyophrenia*.

In all likelihood, this disease stems from a disturbance in the limbic system and in old age exerts its effect over and above those originating in diffuse cortical damage. Much of the latter is caused by cerebro-vascular lesions. Pure senile dementia attributable exclusively to brain atrophy is a comparatively rare disease. Its effects, un-contaminated by those of cerebrovascular accidents, may be best observed in the pre-senile dementias in which the memory deficit is not as prominent a deficit as in the senile psychoses. It tends to set in after some other earlier signs of dementia, which in Alzheimer's disease may in-clude the loss of command over such well-established skills as are exercised in eating, dressing and the habits of cleanliness. In Pick's disease the memory disturbance can be relatively harmless and even completely absent for recent information.

Whether of atrophic or vascular causation, the demen-tias of senility by definition entail disturbances in reason-ing as well as in learning and memory, but the latter are quite prominent and increase progressively in severity. In this respect senile dementia differs from the typical amne-sic syndrome and, as Kral has pointed out, also from the 'benign' forgetfulness of senescence. Kral (1957), who marshals strong evidence for a qualitative distinction be-tween the memory defects of normal ageing and those of senility in which a pathological process is superimposed on the psychological, lists three further differentiating attributes. While senile dementia closely resembles the chronic phase of the amnesic syndrome, the benign forget-fulness of the aged involves neither disorientation, nor memories of personal experiences, nor does it affect primarily recent information. Furthermore, the names or data unavailable on one occasion may be recalled at will on the next. Normal elderly people, one might add, also tend to be aware of their deficiencies in new learning and remembering and indeed often exaggerate the magnitude of their incapacity. On all these counts, the malignant forgetfulness of the elderly, as Kral (1962) calls it, offers a contrast and, in view of the high correlation of its gravity with the patients' mortality, reflects the state of their general health.

Ribot's laws of regression

Although a characteristic of most amnesic disorders is a tendency to remember events and information better the older their memory is, it has been most impressive in cases of senility. Ribot (1882) formulated his first law of regression as the gradual extension of the amnesic disturbance from recent to more distant and then to quite remote memories. The proof of his thesis was based on patients who recovered from amnesic conditions and recaptured their memories in the reverse order. Ribot's law of regression, confirmed by many other clinical observers, has some perplexing implications for the retention of memories. If they were stored in a static form, those held longer could not outlast the recent ones; therefore, retention must involve some dynamic processes. Furthermore, as memory for recent events is lost in senility, it has been observed that previously inaccessible childhood memories become resuscitated. Although they emerge in spontaneous rather than in voluntary recall, some inhibitory influences seem to be released as recent information is forgotten. Several investigators of senile amnesias have disputed the validity of Ribot's law, at least that which specifies the course of temporal regression. For Ribot also listed other gradients of successive stages in amnesic disorders. In content, events are first forgotten, followed by ideas, then by feelings, and last by actions; in language, proper names, common nouns, adjectives and verbs, interjections, and finally gestures are lost in this order; in affect, those disinterested sentiments that are focused on art or science are the first to go, then the ego-altruistic ones, for example sexual love or ambition and last the egoistic, such as fear and anger. The common principle that underlies all these gradients is the regression from the complex and voluntary to the simple and automatic.

Viewing automatic habits as the most completely organized examples of memory, Ribot interpreted his observations as a regression from the least to the most organized. Dugas (1931) fully endorsed this tenet and carried it one step further to the conclusion that the apparent loss of memory entails no quantitative but only a qualitative change, from organized to brute memory – using Bergson's (1911) term. Accordingly Dugas literally equated regression with a return in senility to infantile tastes, attitudes and linguistic habits. Such a retrogression would indeed be facilitated by the sudden re-emergence and prepotence of childhood memories, so that severely confused senile patients may even mistake their own children for their parents, their grandchildren for their brothers and sisters.

The memory and learning disorders of senility

Examples of recent events forgotten in senility overlap widely with those observed in other types of amnesic syndromes, such as the patient's who responded with the appropriate words and show of sorrow to the news of her husband's death but remembered none of it a moment later. Unlike so many amnesic patients, however, the senile are quite talkative and prone to repeat the same story – whether based on a recollection of a childhood experience or on some recent communication – over and over again, and as likely as not to relate it to the very person from whom they had first heard it only a few minutes earlier. Their memory defects are often compounded by dysphasias and apraxias. Apart from these, according to Allison (1962), errors in recalling events in their correct sequence, and of previously familiar places in their true spatial relationships are two characteristic signs of the amnesic syndromes in the elderly. Another two consist of a difficulty in recalling proper names, a disability at times aggravated by perseveration and of an excessive dependence on external cues or on prompting for the retrieval of memories that have been registered and retained.

It would thus seem that the capacity to recall is especially impaired in senility, but Allison, in agreement with most other observers, attributes the memory disturbance primarily to a registration defect. Experimental studies have attempted to isolate the profile of the learning deficit in senile dementia from those characteristic, for example, of the Korsakoff syndrome and of general paresis. According to Gregor (1909), for example, the outstanding impairment in senile dementia is a limited capacity for new learning, especially if literal recall is demanded. The material remembered is reproduced logically, but repeated opportunities to learn show no improvement.

In contrast to Gregor's senile patients, those with Korsakoff's disease increased their learning on repeated trials until they reached a plateau as fatigue set in. They did so notably by correcting their initial errors, but learnt meaningful passages as if they were nonsense, reproducing them in an irrational manner. This tendency they shared with paretic patients who, moreover, displayed severe limitations in new learning, substituting extraneous material for that presented by the experimenter. Repeated tests produced no improvement in their performance, since these patients seemed to be completely impervious to corrections. The amnesic disorder in general paresis extends to distant memories as much or even more damagingly than to the recent, and consequently the former do not provide much fuel for the patients' frequent confabulations. This is a disease that affects reasoning as well as memory and learning and, as in other dementias, in general paresis many errors of recall can be traced to a lack of stable logical connexions between memories.

7 Types of Pathological Memory Disorders

There are few students of amnesic disorders who have not made some attempt to classify those disorders using their own criteria or adopting them from the literature. These attempts are all but necessary to come to terms with the puzzling, often unpredictable and unsystematic, abnormalities that characterize patients with impaired memory function. By separating and redefining those instances in which memory works from those in which it fails, it may be possible to salvage one's faith in the lawfulness of human nature, a faith that is in danger of collapsing when faced with the actual phenomena of amnesic derangements. Furthermore, identifying and isolating the disorders of memory and learning observed in a patient is a necessary preliminary to diagnosis, prognosis, and treatment. The contribution of these endeavours in classification to a theory of memory and learning may be incidental but is not negligible.

The broadest distinction in the realm of memory disorders is that between amnesias and paramnesias. The former embrace all instances in which information that has once been known or that normally would be registered is lost or unavailable; the latter cover the varieties of memory distortion. In contrast to the negative symptoms of amnesia and hypomnesia, the paramnesias have been referred to as the positive symptoms of memory disturbance. The same epithet would also apply to those instances of hypermnesia, of abnormally detailed or vivid recollections of events, that characterize certain mental diseases, drug-induced disorders and – reputedly – the critical moments of death or survival in drowning and other mortal dangers.

A widely accepted principle of classifying memory disorders is their aetiology, for example, psychogenic versus neurogenic, subdividing the latter into surgical ablations, cerebral tumours, vascular accidents, degenerative processes, intracranial infection, anoxia, metabolic and toxic disturbances including alcoholic intoxication, nutritional deficiency, epileptic seizures. Another principle of classification is based on the duration of the disturbance. Transient amnesias constitute one pole, the relatively stable or progressively deteriorating chronic amnesic syndromes the opposite pole, with recurrent episodes and longer lasting but reversible disturbances occupying the middle. To some extent classifications according to the last two criteria are interdependent; the senile amnesias of degenerative aetiology are always chronic, epileptic disturbances are characteristically episodic, some toxic disorders are apt to be reversible, but most known causes of transient amnesias – alcohol, anoxia, vitamin B deficiency, vascular occlusions – can also result in permanent damage.

Amnesias

Animal experimenters habitually report as instances of amnesia their rat's or cat's failure to reproduce on cue an experimentally acquired aversive or appetitive response. While amnesia in man refers to the forgetting of all kinds of information, including some learned behaviour that does not lend itself to verbal coding, many clinicians restrict the term to describe a patient's inability to remember personal experiences. In accordance with this usage, the apraxias, agnosias and aphasias are customarily treated as distinct disorders – a custom that will be observed here – even though they may be closely associated with and stem from much the same basic functional impairment as the amnesias. The apraxic patient's inability to execute an action plan has a close parallel in the amnesic patient's inability to complete the operations necessary for the retrieval of a memory, as does the failure to find the required word in nominal aphasia. Jargon aphasia, like confabulation, can be viewed as a disturbance in recognition, that is, in recognizing the inappropriateness of one's response. Some examples of partial amnesia reported in the literature are hard to distinguish from apraxias and agnosias, for example, those limited to one sensory modality, to one side of the body, to all musical knowledge.

Retrograde amnesia

Severe and enduring memory disorders involve the forgetting of information that used to be well under the patient's command prior to his illness. The most striking, but by no means the only, examples of retrograde amnesia are those that affect the patient's personal experiences, the salient data and conditions of his past life, for example, his marriage, children, jobs, places where he lived. The content of memories unavailable for voluntary recall or for accurate recognition can either be determined by temporal boundaries, for example, the year before the onset of the disturbance, or by some emotional criterion such as events and data relating to a particular person who, in certain cases, happens to be the patient himself.

Retrograde amnesia is rarely complete in the sense that all memories dating from a given period of the patient's life history or connected with a person or experience that seems to be forgotten in its essentials are entirely out of the range of recall or recognition. Apart from the islands in the sea of amnesia, some such memories may emerge spontaneously, or indeed be available for voluntary recall on some occasions although not on others. All this suggests that retrograde amnesia is a dysfunction in recall or recognition. It certainly is not a defect in registration or learning, since the events or information affected were once securely remembered. Retrograde amnesia could, however, also stem from deranged retention, since some data about and from the past – and in many patients a great deal of them – may forever remain outside the boundaries of recovery.

In chronic memory disorders retrograde amnesia is subject to fluctuations but remains substantially stable in its extent, except in so far as it would expand apace with a general dementing process. In transient and relatively short-term amnesic disturbances, for example, following brain surgery or concussion, the retrograde amnesia usually contracts progressively until only the events that closely preceded the traumatic incident may remain affected. Those events will never be recalled as are other personal experiences although details about them can be learned from informants; they may reappear as some dreamlike recollection or may be elicited under hypnosis. They were properly perceived but not fully registered and for that reason differ from memories that had been accurately recalled before they became inaccessible. This difference furnishes the rationale for distinguishing the *retroactive amnesias* of a few seconds' or minutes' extent from the *retrograde amnesias*. The distinction does not imply that in retrograde amnesia memories are lost; they may only be difficult of access, but they had gone through those processes of consolidation, or coding and filing, that are necessary to render information available for future recall, while in retroactive amnesia those processes were not completed.

Anterograde amnesia

Many memory disorders start with an episode of confusion or complete unconsciousness. Events that take place during that period are obviously not registered, although the patient may carry out quite intricate action plans so that his condition appears to be normal. To the examples furnished by the boxing ring and football field can be added others from horsemanship and at least one from the operating room: the case of a surgeon who in a state of post-traumatic amnesia following a head injury directed a colleague to trephine his skull. Post-traumatic amnesias usually clear up within a few hours or days, although residual defects can be detected even weeks after the accident. Other examples of anterograde amnesia, also described as *progressive* or *continuous amnesia* and *amnesia of fixation*, persist for the remainder of the patient's life.

In its severest form, anterograde amnesia entails a seemingly complete incapacity of learning, yet most patients manage to acquire some new information although it may not amount to much: a face or two, a name, the way to the lavatory, one's bed on the ward. The impairment affects memory for life experiences as well as for formal learning. The patients may recollect virtually nothing they have done or thought or that had happened to them over periods of years; they register none of the changes that have occurred in their lives or in the world outside, such as births or deaths in the family, the outbreak of a war, or a new government. The universe seems to have come to a stop when their illness started, or rather some time before that, and they are not aware of having aged since. Persons they remember – husband or wife, children, more seldom a friend – also appear to them at the age they last saw them before their breakdown. Obsolete fashions and styles are preserved with greater fidelity for not having been superseded by others in the patient's memory but – since chronic anterograde amnesia is always associated with retrograde amnesia – the reconstruction of the past is patchy, confused, and at least partly inaccurate.

Experientially there is a complete gap for the period covered by anterograde amnesia; the present moment – no matter how many years have passed – may be felt as if it followed immediately upon the last moment of consciousness prior to the amnesic breakdown. If the patient is aware of a gap between the two occasions, he cannot fill it or even recognize a few landmarks in the empty space. He is grossly disoriented in time and if he should name the day's date correctly when asked to, he would produce a piece of information entirely isolated from all personal experiences. Without a firm stance in the present, his temporal disorientation stretches far beyond the onset of his illness so that past memories are apt to become jumbled –

displaced from their true chronological order. They may retain their true sequential positions but become displaced *en bloc*, or condensed into a narrower span of time than that which they had actually occupied. These errors of temporal placement occur alike in the recall of personal and of public events, and belong rather within the patient's retrograde than his anterograde amnesia.

Disorientation for time, place and persons is a salient feature of the confusional phase that marks the beginning of many amnesic disorders. The concussed football player who carries on the game with skill and verve may turn against his own goal and tackle his own team mates. The patient on the ward is quite likely to mistake his surroundings for a rooming house, for example, and cast his fellow patients, nurses and doctors into roles that fit such a setting.

With transient amnesias the disorientation clears up completely. If the anterograde amnesia becomes chronic, this derangement persists in a much attenuated form. Patients are indeed apt to lose their bearings, but often learn their way about the hospital grounds and can also learn that the place they live in is a mental hospital. After a while they recognize at least some of the doctors, orderlies and fellow patients for what they are, but this learning is quite precarious. Unfamiliar faces may be mistaken for familiar ones and those seen many times are apt to be misplaced, particularly into a social setting known from before the onset of the illness.

Much of this disorientation is clearly secondary to the anterograde amnesia, and that seems to be entirely a defect in registration, in processing the incoming information so as to make it available for future reference. Quite a few authors have stated the opinion that anterograde amnesia, especially if transient, is purely and simply attributable to impaired registration. Others have quoted instances of latent learning, of patients who were unable to repeat a message or who appeared to have instantly forgotten some incident, yet reproduced the message accurately or spontaneously referred to the incident at some later date. These are incontestably examples of faulty recall; they are also exceptions to a general rule. Far more often than not the information that is unavailable to him for immediate recall remains so for the rest of the amnesic patient's life. He absorbs abnormally small amounts of the surrounding events or of messages presented to him for learning and forgets even those small amounts at a much faster rate than do normal people.

Forgetting is not a unitary process. Quite apart from the common examples in which parts or certain features of the memory are retained, there are cases in which some instruction or rule may be recalled verbally but not be manifest in action or, in reverse, an experience may show its impact on subsequent behaviour but not be recollected as a distinct memory. Amnesic patients provide some remarkable instances of both these types of partial remembering. They may, for example, learn a sequential pattern in an experimental task well enough to recite it but nevertheless be unable to execute the task in accordance with that pattern. Ranschburg's (1911) patient exemplified a similar paradox, when she correctly stated that, following a lumbar puncture she had just undergone, she would have to lie on her back for twenty-four hours, yet got up later in spite of her nurse's protestations and denied that there was any particular reason for her to stay in bed.

More common on the ward is the opposite type of dissociation as reported by Janet (1903) for example, whose patient denied having ever received E.C.T. before but showed considerable anxiety when the shock apparatus was brought into his room. Claparède (1951) illustrated this anomaly experimentally when, shaking hands with a patient, he jabbed her with a pin hidden in his fingers. A few minutes later he reached out his hand to her again but she refused to take it. Asked for an explanation, the patient answered that she was afraid that her hand might be hurt with a needle but seemed to be completely unaware that this is precisely what had happened to her. All she would admit was that people do sometimes conceal pins in their hands.

Still another variety of partial remembering was exemplified by Williams and Smith's (1954) patient after he had recovered from an amnesic syndrome that originated in tuberculous meningitis. When shown a photograph of a group of young men, his colleagues in a training programme taken shortly before his illness, he could name them all but had no idea of where he had met them. These anomalies are indisputably attributable to impaired recall. In the last case there is no reason for suspecting any defect in registration; although in the other instances quoted the experiences inaccessible to recall may well have been insufficiently coded and filed for future recollection. The numerous occasions of grave retention defects over quite short spans of time that have been observed in amnesic patients furnish a clear indication of impaired registration. This impairment may result in cumulative effects if recall, too, is disordered, as indeed it is in patients who are afflicted with a retrograde as well as an anterograde amnesia.

The joint presence of a deficit in registration and in recall suggests that a function common to both these processes is impaired and that its derangement may also account for the amnesic patient's poverty of affect and lack of spontaneity. A function manifested in the setting up and execution of action plans, without the cues provided by biological needs or overlearned habits, might supply an explanation. It would also account for the amnesic patients' failures to correct the most palpable and often quite incredible errors in recall.

Paramnesias

Patients with memory disorders are notable alike for their failures to recall events or data that would normally be remembered and for making gross errors in their purported recollection of the past. Causal connexions between the two types of anomaly are plausible enough: the absence or unavailability of the correct memory could provide an occasion for a *pseudo-reminiscence*, or conversely, a failure to recognize an illusory memory as such and to sift it out would bar access to the true memory.

The most obvious examples of paramnesia are false recollections based on no actual event in the past. Such pseudo-reminiscences can be entirely the products of invention, that is pure fabrications, or be based on dreams, or be derived from the histories of other, true or fictional, characters. There may be a factual core in the false recollection, but this is blown up and embellished beyond all likeness to the original event. Scheid (1934), among several episodes of a transatlantic voyage with an amnesic patient, reported an occasion when the patient attempted to buy a beer at the bar of the lounge but the barman, on the doctor's instruction, courteously but firmly refused to serve him. The patient reported the incident as one he had dreamt but also with a more dramatic conclusion: having been refused the beer he was forcibly thrown out of the lounge. He may indeed have been afraid that this might happen to him and in recollection confused fact and fantasy. The material used to elaborate and reshape an actual memory can be drawn from imagination, from another person's history or from the patient's own past reaching into an entirely different phase and setting of his life.

False recollections are not only the products of errors in content or context. Personal memories involve a twofold reference, to the past and to oneself, and both these references are liable to become deranged. Past events can be experienced as ongoing, that which happened once as recurrent, the present as a repetition of an identical previous experience. The actions and sayings of others can be mistaken for one's own and one's own words can be ascribed to another person.

False recollections

False recollections are very common and quite normal in small children who have not learned yet how or when to discriminate the data of observation from those of fantasy. In adults – unless at the service of artistic creation – they constitute a pathological sign and are characteristic of certain abnormal personalities or mental diseases.

Psychopathic personalities who otherwise are not notable for memory disorders habitually blend truth with fiction and very likely do so without full awareness. Their compulsive tendency to invent stories or to make false statements is a symptom known in the literature as *pseudologia fantastica*, in which, however, the fictitious memories are not held so firmly as to be immune to disproof by rational demonstration. False recollections form a sizable portion of paranoid delusions and of the self-deprecatory memories in depression. They are also symptomatic of schizophrenic patients who are apt to report autobiographical data heard from others as their own. A propensity to annex the exploits of other real or fictitious characters to one's own life history is typical of alcohol addicts and of the paretic, for whom such appropriations serve the purpose of self aggrandizement, supply material for bragging.

False recollections, as shown in Chapter 1, are particularly common in testimony. Many defendants charged with homicide or murder have no recollection whatever of the crime, especially if it was committed in a state of deranged consciousness. Sometimes they confess to having acted under compulsion, quite unaware that the source of the compulsion was in themselves – an alternate personality. Often the amnesias and paramnesias brought up in their defence are faked but they can be so implausible that their deliberate fabrication seems quite improbable. Hopwood and Snell (1933) quote the case of a man who had shot his sister and then failed in a suicide attempt. On questioning, he stated that he and his sister had gone for a walk and he had taken a gun to shoot a rabbit, but found none and therefore had not fired his gun. They met two men in the field, who first shot him and then his sister, and the last he remembered was seeing his sister lying on the ground.

A special type of paramnesia distinguished and described by Kraepelin (1887) is the *associative pseudo-reminiscence*. This occurs when seeing or hearing about a person, a patient falsely recollects having met him somewhere before or having done something with him. It is not always a straightforward decision to distinguish these purely respondent from the simple or emitted pseudo-reminiscences. Sorting out truth from invention or one source of false recollection from another also presents serious difficulties. According to Kraepelin, false recollections based on dreams or hallucinations are stable over repeated occasions while illusions of memory derived from a factual source tend to be variable. The repeated recall of a pseudo-reminiscence, however, may also stabilize its content. Like healthy people, patients with memory disorders are apt to relate their false recollections with some diffidence at first but as they repeatedly tell their tale their belief in its truth becomes firmer.

Confabulation

Patients with disturbed memory function are not aware of the full extent of their amnesia. At first they may not be aware of it at all and would regard it as absurd as would any normal person that they should not remember where they had lived the year before or what they had done an hour ago. If asked, they will give an answer and their answers are often self-contradictory as well as factually incorrect. They supply most of the material that is described as confabulation.

The term is not restricted to this type of false auto-biographical reporting. It has been used to refer to the various types of pseudo-reminiscences described in the previous section as well as to deliberate and imaginative fabrications. French authors in particular are careful to distinguish mythomania, the invention of fantastic tales, from the more homely yarns spun in confabulation and to further distinguish confabulation that fills a gap in memory from other examples of fabulation or fabrication.

Filling a gap in the patient's personal memory is indeed the typical occasion for a confabulation. Such a definition, however, is ambiguous in that it may be understood as entailing the patient's awareness of such a gap and his deliberate invention or borrowing of some material to fill it. This would be a serious misconstruction of the cir-cumstances that elicit confabulations and would hardly be compatible with the observation that, unlike other false recollections, confabulations can be provoked by the interviewer. The way this happens could not be described better than was done by Ross (1890) almost eight decades ago.

An infirmary patient of my own, who lay helpless in bed for nine weeks, narrated day by day to us how he had been out walking on the same morning. To the usual question of 'Where have you been today?' he would reply, 'Oh, I have been out to the Pier. It was blowing quite fresh, but it has done me good.' 'Have you had anything to drink?' 'Oh, yes; I met a friend. I forget his name, but I know him quite well, and we went to a public house and had three-penny-worth of whisky each.' On another day he described himself as having been walking in Whalley, of which district I believe he was a native, and he never failed to praise the beauty of the country, or to meet a friend with whom he had the inevitable three-penny-worth of whisky.

Except for the rise in the cost of whisky, this dialogue could be replicated from any number of hospitals that care for amnesic patients. Brodmann (1902) reported an interview with a Korsakoff patient who had been in a Frankfurt hospital continuously for the previous two months.

'What have you been doing today?' 'We went over to Sachsenhausen where we inspected some goods, and then travelled to Bockenheim where we had breakfast, and then went to church. It is a holiday for Catholics [untrue]. After that I drank a bottle of wine with an old friend; one always finds good company at our regular tavern. Then I looked in at home for a moment, saw the wife and children. My wife has been sick for such a long time now, and then I came here to your office.'

Since the patient was a customs official, the inspection of goods would be as routine an occupation for him as drinking wine at the Bockenheim inn on a holiday. In fact he had attended to his duties – as well as he could – right up to the day before his hospitalization, but his wife had been dead for four years.

A second episode, dating a few months later from the same patient's record, throws light on some other aspects of confabulations that are typical of the amnesic syndrome. It was an occasion on which the patient managed to remember the goal of his endeavours, perhaps because it bore on a fixed concern of his for a medical certificate of leave.

He was told to fetch it from his office. Without a moment's reflection that his office was not in the building, he set out immediately and was not deterred by finding himself in the watch room. He went from one room to another, and finally returned reporting without the least embarrassment that the certificate of leave was no longer in his office, as earlier that morning he had personally handed it to the Chief Inspector who had given him permission to stay away from work. In all these instances [comments Brodmann] there is evidence of that confabulation so characteristic of patients whose memory for the immediately foregoing is missing; they answer questions with fabrications invented on the spot in order to cover up their momentary uncertainty or their lack of memory. These patients are never at a loss for a reply, they round out or counterfeit reality with keen inventiveness from their imagination, and without ever becoming aware of their falsifications.

It is an apt description but for the emphasis on inventiveness and imagination. In fact in the instances quoted and in most others the source of the confabulatory material is the patient's own past. Genuine experiences are transposed in time to explain away or round out the incoherencies of the immediate past or, for that matter, of a forgotten or faintly remembered episode of the remote past. The patient's disorientation in time, in his physical and social setting, aids these errors in chronological and situational placement as much as his tolerance of contradiction abets their flow.

A disability to make comparisons between objects presented consecutively is probably at the root of the amnesic patient's 'lack of critical attitude'. As the patient's disorientation recedes, his propensity to confabulate also diminishes. There are considerable individual differences in this respect, and the degree of insight into the memory disorder is probably a decisive factor. At any rate, confabulation is always present in the early confusional stage of an amnesic syndrome but may disappear completely from the chronic patient's behaviour and give way to an extraordinary readiness to admit ignorance. Questions about the onset of the patient's illness are the most likely to elicit a confabulatory explanation and typically the mention of an earlier illness or accident that had no causal connexion with the patient's present infirmity.

Errors in reference

The impression that a completely new experience is the replicate of an earlier one is familiar to normal and healthy people, but is far more common in those with some memory disorder, especially with temporal lobe seizures. The most familiar version of this paramnesia occurs in visual perception and is known as *déjà vu,* but it has its counterpart in other sense modalities, in thought, and in general experience. Janet (1942) declared that *déjà vu* is an anomaly, not of memory, but of perception, being essentially a negation of the present nature of an event rather than an affirmation of its pastness. People with memory disorders evidently cannot be satisfied with a simple dichotomy of the familiar and the new. Quite apart from their diffidence in assigning a person, object or situation to one class or another, they seem to recognize a meaningful third category. Syz's (1937) patient, for example, when taken back to his room remarked, 'I cannot say that I have been here already, but the room is not totally foreign to me.'

Déjà vu in healthy people is an isolated phenomenon; in epileptic patients it may become recurrent and cases have been reported in which it had become a chronic disorder. An example in point was Pick's (1876) patient who remarked that 'from that time on almost every job I did in my business appeared familiar to me, as if I had done it before years ago, in the same order and under exactly the same circumstances ... everything that happened about me evoked this impression. At times I became conscious of it the very moment of perception, or a few minutes or hours later and often only the following day.'

Kraepelin also discussed a paramnesia related to *déjà vu* and greatly favoured by novelists, the *pseudo-presentiments*, as they occurred in patients with memory derangements. In these hallucinations of memory, events as they happen are experienced as if they had been foretold in a dream or a warning and thus been known in every detail before their onset. Kraepelin (1887) referred to these paramnesias of temporal reference as *identifying pseudo-reminiscences*.

The fact that they are particularly prone to follow an epileptic discharge, which interrupts the normal activity of the brain, supports the view that *déjà vu* and similar anomalies result from an interruption of the perceptual process so that it splits into a past as well as another current experience. That a unitary and continuous event can become divided into a series of experientially discrete memories is immediately apparent in the symptom of *reduplicative paramnesia*. Patients with chronic memory disturbances often believe that, for example, a first medical examination of its kind is the repetition of an earlier one by the same physician and also experience their continued hospitalization as something new every time their attention is drawn to it. Cameron (1940) described another type of reduplicative memory disturbance when he reported that senile amnesic patients may recall after an hour a room with one bed, two windows and four chairs as containing four beds, eight windows and sixteen chairs.

The opposite to the *déjà vu* or *déjà entendu* is the *jamais vu* or *jamais entendu* phenomenon, an example of total failure in recognition. A special case of this type of anomaly arises when someone relates as his own doing the action of another or prints as his own the words originally spoken or written by someone else. Such plagiarism can be entirely innocent and be perpetrated by perfectly sane people in isolated instances. In senility it occurs quite regularly and as a clinical symptom has been known as *cryptomesia*.

While the appropriation of another person's actions or sayings is a fairly usual occurrence, the reverse misattribution is rare. *Projection* can be observed quite commonly in normal people as well as in psychopathological cases, but that typically entails the attribution of an intent rather than a completed act or statement to an outsider. Children accused of some misdemeanour, adults facing a charge in the dock or if they are politicians making speeches, are apt to blame friends or enemies for their own culpable actions. To some extent such charges may be nourished by unconscious false recollections but most of them are deliberate lies. Amnesic patients may confusedly credit others with the execution of some perfectly harmless deeds of their own but this is not a very common type of paramnesia, largely because those patients remember little of past actions or pronouncements and what they do recall tends to be closely related to themselves.

I witnessed a striking example of the misattribution of one's own achievement in recall to an interlocutor, when on one occasion I asked a man afflicted with an amnesic syndrome some questions relating to his brothers. The older brother had been killed in a road accident some months before the patient's illness. The younger was about to get married in a foreign country. The details asked for thus included both data that may not have been properly registered and others that were quite clearly registered and with a powerful emotional impact, but which the patient seemed to have forgotten, for the day before our interview he mistakenly believed that the mail had brought a letter from his brother who had in fact been dead for some time.

In response to my detailed but entirely uninformative questions, the patient divulged his knowledge of his brother's fatal accident and correctly named all the circumstances that attended it, as well as all of the details I had asked about the forthcoming wedding. Since he was aware of and profoundly worried about his memory disorder, I promptly complimented him on this successful performance in recall, but he did not accept my reassurance for he was convinced that all the information he had given me had in fact just been imparted by me to him. Half an hour later we repeated the entire performance. I asked the same questions, he gave me the same correct answers and again I drew his attention to the fact that he had just managed to recall a number of details about his brother's accident and about his other brother's wedding. Again he remained unconvinced and under the impression that I had just apprised him of those events in his family.

To be unaware of having just reported some personally significant information and to believe that one has just been the recipient of all that information is a very unusual example of paramnesia. In this instance the misattribution of a factually and contextually correct performance in recall to the interlocutor is most likely to have been caused by the structure of the interview in which I programmed the patient's responses step by step with the questions I addressed to him. His performance may thus have been akin to that of a hypnotic subject obeying an instruction, or one of Penfield's patients (cf. p. 113) whose motor responses or recollections were elicited by direct electrical stimulation of the exposed cortex. He evidently did not recognize his performance as his own but had registered accurately enough the transaction that had taken place between us and reconstructed it in the only manner that made sense to him.

This interpretation of a most unusual paramnesia reaffirms the crucial part played by the patient's incapacity to programme action sequences in the amnesic syndrome. The recollection was false neither in content nor in its setting. The patient's disavowal of his active participation and his consequent assumption of a purely receptive role could hardly be explained by such motivational determinants as are at the root of projection. In order to distinguish the type of error in recall just described from other varieties of paramnesia I gave it the name *probole*, the Greek equivalent of projection which, however, carries no motivational connotation.

8 Evaluation and Treatment

Although memory is an important function, tests of memory play a relatively small part in clinical assessment, nor is there much that can be done to help people who are impaired in that function. Clinical tests of memory are used at times for differential diagnosis but dispositions are more likely to be made on the basis of interviews or situational cues. Tests may be used to verify a patient's complaints that his memory is deteriorating and often enough fail to confirm his impression, but for all that do not convince him that all is well. They provide the most useful service in controlled evaluations of changes in memory function, whether as a result of a treatment or of some natural process, by furnishing comparable data on successive occasions. Naturally, any change observed between the successive tests can be evaluated only against data obtained over a similar interval from appropriately matched control subjects, who do not undergo the experimental treatment or other process that is under investigation.

Since performance both in learning and in remembering involves several processes each of which could be impaired independently or to a different degree from the others, no single technique can be employed as a test of either function. There are standardized tests of memory, composed of several tasks, that have the merit of probing more than a single process but spoil this virtue by producing a single composite score. The memory quotient thus obtained may be of some use when set against the patient's intelligence quotient, but is of little help for clinical diagnosis or, indeed, for a definition of the patient's memory disorder. These goals are far more effectively served by the employment of appropriately chosen experimental tests and interviews, neither of which allow for comparisons with population norms or of a specific clinical test of memory that has been standardized on various samples drawn from the patient population and on healthy people as well.

Tests of Memory

Of the composite memory tests the most widely used is Wechsler's (1945) Memory Scale. Like the same author's Intelligence Scale it consists of several subtests and these are:

1 Questions probing *personal and current information*, e.g. 'How old are you?' 'Who is the Mayor of this city?'
2 Questions probing *orientation*, e.g. 'What year is this?' 'What is the name of this place you are in?'
3 Tests of *mental control* such as counting backward from twenty to one, or reciting the alphabet.
4 *Tests of logical memory* by immediate recall of two short narrative passages read to the subject, scored by the number of content units reproduced.
5 *Digit span* forward and in reverse, as in Wechsler's Intelligence Scale.
6 *Reproduction* by drawing of three symmetrical designs immediately after an exposure of ten seconds.
7 *Paired-associate learning*.

Like some older omnibus tests of memory, Wechsler's is standardized only with regard to the over-all score, additively derived from its subtests. For diagnostic purposes it would be more useful to draw a profile of the subtest scores but, since no standards of comparison have been established, psychologists often find it more expedient to devise their own batteries, including in them tasks that sample a larger variety of performances in learning and remembering. Williams (1967) has constructed a battery of five tests that instead of compounding scores obtained from disparate tasks aims at a profile of weighted scores. It includes the following items:

1 *Digit span* forwards and backwards.
2 The *Rey-Davis learning test*: four square boards with three rows of three pegs. Eight pegs are loose and the one fixed is in a different position on each board. The task is to learn the positions of the pegs that cannot be lifted from their sockets.
3 *Word-learning test*: learning the definition of unfamiliar words.
4 *Delayed recall* of nine objects shown as pictures after a lapse of seven to ten minutes. If the subject cannot recall all of them, he is helped first by prompting questions and, after a further failure, by a recognition test in which he is shown drawings of twenty-five objects including the nine presented for recall.
5 *Memory for personal events*, i.e., questions about the subject's early childhood, middle youth, late youth, 21st birthday, and recent past, e.g. 'Can you describe your first school?' 'How did you spend last Christmas?'

In her previous studies of amnesic patients, Williams (1953) made excellent use of recognition tests which also furnished graded clues, by showing the object to be remembered first as an amorphous blot and subsequently in shapes approximating by steps the drawing of an articulate object. Hers is an example well worth observing in the design of memory tests. They should include performance by recognition as well as by recall and explore the information retained by means of prompting or similar aids. It is also valuable for providing a non-verbal test of memory, as do the Rey-Davis pegboards. The latter, however, are of limited applicability, for Zangwill (1943), who has carefully investigated this test and classified the types of errors that can be made in its performance, does not regard it as suitable for patients with a high I.Q. A qualitative analysis of the errors has been found to have diagnostic significance in the reproduction of line drawings as well, in Benton's (1955), and in Graham and Kendall's (1960) tests for example, especially for the screening of structural brain damage.

Tests of learning are selected or designed so as to determine the type, the amount or the complexity of the material that is within the patient's range of mastery. The number of trials or time needed to achieve a criterion of learning is of less importance in the study of impaired function than it is in the study of normal function, largely because most patients with memory disorders hardly benefit from repeated exposures to the material or from additional time. Learning tests extend over a wide variety of tasks from the acquisition of conditioned responses and manual skills to the learning of verbal material logically or by rote. The problem at hand may not indicate an exploration over this entire range of performances, but as a rule it is desirable to test learning and memory with information presented through more than one sensory channel, the auditory and the kinesthetic as well as the visual. This consideration is of particular importance when the localization of a lesion presents a diagnostic problem.

The learning and reproduction after no delay, as well as after delays of varying lengths, of stories or other narrative texts is usually an appropriate test of learning and memory with patients. Lists of unconnected natural words or nonsense syllables also serve as tests of learning and of immediate and short-term memory, and, like the stories, can be presented aurally or visually. The digit span is widely used to assess short-term retention, although it tests concentration rather than memory. More informative about memory function is the running digit span which presents strings of digits that exceed the subject's immediate retention span, but with the instruction to repeat only a given number of the terminal items, observing the order of presentation.

Of necessity, most tests of memory probe retention only over relatively short intervals, typically immediately after first presentation or the last learning trial and then perhaps again a few minutes, an hour or two hours later, but during the same testing session. Performance in life situations, however, is more faithfully simulated by tests of recall or recognition after much longer intervals when the continuity of the test situation and its corresponding task-set have been interrupted for some days or weeks and the environmental cues are no longer present. Performance in delayed recall – whether after five minutes or a year – must, naturally enough, be weighed against success in original learning and in that regard patients with memory disorder can only rarely be equated with control subjects.

Tests of learning, those that involve the acquisition of a skill or of a map no less than verbal tasks, allow for the estimation of retention by relearning as well as by recall, reproduction or recognition. Some of the original learning is almost invariably lost with time and intervening events, so that several re-learning trials may be needed to reach the level of proficiency attained in original learning. The difference between the number of trials on first and on second (or any subsequent) occasions gives a measure of *savings*, and this has in several studies of amnesic patients shown retention when tests of delayed recall showed none; so may tests of recognition which, moreover, allow for a wider choice of sensory channels of presentation than tests of recall. Naturally enough, whenever performance is defective it is necessary to ascertain the extent to which an impairment of sensory-perceptual or executive functions contributes to the defect. Tests of learning and memory must therefore be supplemented with evaluations of receptor and effector functions and such processes as, for example, organizing the incoming data, searching, matching, planning and completing plans may also be effectively studied in perceptual or motor tasks.

Alongside suitable standardized performance tests, the interview remains an essential tool for probing memory disorders. It is virtually the only method for investigating long-term memory, that is, the retention of old memories and early learning. The content is selected primarily from personal experience, for example the first day at school, the parental home, the wedding day, etc. Usually it is quite difficult or indeed impossible to verify the accuracy of the answer, or to help with cues if no answer is forthcoming. Questions about salient public events would therefore be preferable, but there are immense differences among people in the interest they take in politics, sports, or war news, for example. Interviews can be used to probe recent as well as old memories, covering alike public and private events. They are undoubtedly the most effective means to determine a patient's orientation in time, place and towards persons, especially those he has met since the onset of his disorder, and the extent of his retroactive and post-traumatic amnesia. A topic of special interest for interviews is the subject's recollection of previous questions, of the themes discussed or of tests he took earlier in the session.

Answers obtained in interviews are rated primarily for the amount and accuracy of the information given, but they can be submitted to further scrutiny, for example, for a qualitative analysis of the gaps in the content and of the attempts, if any, to fill such gaps. While tests of learning and memory aim at quantitive scores, there, too, qualitative analyses of the responses are likely to be informative about the process and disturbances characteristic of a patient and these can be standardized. Criteria of for example, sharpening, importation, assimilation to personal needs and concerns, etc., can be established in advance and an example that fits each category can then be tallied from the records of the patient's response.

Correcting Disorders

The treatment of learning defects forms an important topic of educational psychology, but a discussion of the special techniques explored and of the reasons advanced for their application is out of place here. Remedial action is indicated especially when a student performs at a level of proficiency far below his capacity inferred from performance in other subjects or from extra-curricular observations. Accordingly, the remedial programme is to train him in special skills or to arouse his interest and motivation for mastery.

Disorders of learning manifested at school frequently appear to stem from the student's refusal to recognize the standards and goals set by the educational system and the roots of such rebellion or resistance, in turn, may reach into a troubled domestic situation. Much of the school counsellors' efforts is directed at sorting out and resolving the conflicts between the student's and society's value systems or the tangled interpersonal relations that interfere with the student's scholastic progress. These interventions by psychiatrists and other professional persons as well as by counsellors often help students with learning problems. The successes thus achieved are perhaps enough to explain why accounts of such interventions should occupy so large a portion of the literature devoted to the treatment of learning disorders, but the uncritical reader of so many enthusiastic case reports might be tempted to oversimplify the problem.

The case reports describe how the disentanglement and resolution or examination of an interpersonal conflict – for example, the neglect of the child by the parents, their unconscious opposition to his success at school, their marital disharmony – suddenly results in improved scholastic performance. They rarely give adequate consideration to other likely relevant factors or mention that in numberless instances similar or even graver domestic situations and conflicts do not prevent the boy or girl from performing well at school. The psychological problems under discussion are therefore hardly sufficient causes of the learning disability. The other causes may of course be unknown or, if known, be less amenable to correction unless they happen to be cases of, for example, nutritional deficiency, certain visual or auditory defects, or dyslexia.

Learning disorders in adulthood apart from those manifested in the symptoms of psychiatric diseases consist of the inability or insufficient ability to acquire new skills. Techniques to enliven the learner's flagging interest and others designed to utilize and transfer his pre-existing skills are effective as remedial devices. While they all follow certain common basic principles, the method must obviously be chosen and adapted to the specific problem at hand. The basic principles for improving the acquisition of motor skills also apply to verbal learning, where help by providing mediators, by spelling out rules for organizing the input and for breaking it up into portions that do not exceed the attention span can be spelled out more explicitly.

In his excellent chapter on improving memory, Hunter (1957) concludes that, past the phase of learning, nothing can be done about it; there is no known device by which retention or remembering can be improved, and that mere practice like physical exercise undertaken to strengthen muscles will not improve the capacity to learn. In regard to defective learning and memory the case may be modified somewhat, especially if the problem is the relearning of a previously well-established skill, like speech after a stroke with dysphasic effects or writing after the paralysis of the dominant hand. In some cases relearning must go through the same laborious slow stages as original learning but having reached a certain level of proficiency the pace of recovery may accelerate or indeed all the remaining lost capacity may return at a single stroke. This happened with a young man described by Ribot (1882) who had lost his spoken and written vocabulary and had to relearn both, first in French and later in Latin, all by the laborious slow stages that he had gone through at school. One day, as he was engaged in these studies, he suddenly exclaimed 'I have a strange feeling that I have known all this before.' From that moment on he rapidly regained his lost language skills.

More dramatic still is the case reported by Righetti (1920) of a man who had fired a pistol, first at his sister-in-law and then at himself, and had failed alike in his attempt at homicide and suicide. The bullet damaged the tip of the man's right temporal lobe and the adjacent area of the frontal lobe. Traumatic amnesia affected the entire incident with the gun and extended some distance before and after as well. While hospitalized, superimposed on this memory loss, the patient developed a retrograde amnesia that spread over a month preceding his injury. His retrograde amnesia persisted until, two years and three months following the accident, the patient recalled in a dream the circumstances that had led to his injury and with that dream experience recovered in his waking state all the memories affected by the retrograde amnesia.

There is no technique by which the content of normal dreams can be prescribed, but the type of amnesia that disabled Righetti's patient is quite responsive to hypnotic or psychotherapeutic treatment. Hysteric amnesias, according to Parfitt and Gall (1944), yield to mere persuasion, without hypnosis or narcosis, as does also malingering. In contrast, only barbiturate hypnosis succeeded in eliciting information within the range of retroactive amnesia in several of Russell and Nathan's (1946) traumatic patients. Anamnestic drugs are widely used with the desired results, but they seem to be quite ineffective with chronic amnesic patients. Brain surgery can successfully restore some types of severe memory disturbance, originating in the mechanical obstruction of a cortical pathway, even after several months' duration, but has as yet not been tried for relieving amnesic disorders associated with subcortical lesions.

Claims have been made for the improvement of memory function and learning in senile and pre-senile patients by the administration of R N A, or of drugs that allegedly stimulate R N A synthesis in the brain (cf. p. 82), but lack the support of evidence from independent and controlled studies. It would seem on *a priori* considerations that the more closely the mental defect is associated with an irreversible tissue damage in the brain and the older the lesion, the smaller is the likelihood of the defects being reparable by pharmacological means.

By and large, the more severe the memory disturbance the less can be done to relieve it by any technique – surgical, chemical or psychological. Prosthetic devices, such as written reminders, calendars, diaries may help the healthy person who does not trust his memory, or ageing people who begin to suffer from some deterioration. They may even prove useful to some patients with severe memory disturbance who are aware of their incapacity, but typically amnesic patients have little insight into their condition, and are as ineffective in those searching and checking operations that the employment of such devices involves as they are in learning and remembering. If it is disappointing to admit that, with so many seemingly scholarly treatises on mnemotechnics on the shelves of our libraries, no one reliable technique can be recommended to help patients with memory disorders, let us be comforted by Mark Twain's anecdote about the memory expert who astounded his audience by remembering hundreds of names and faces but, at the end of his lecture, walked out into the rain forgetting his umbrella.

References

Albert, D. J. (1966a), 'The effect of spreading depression on the consolidation of learning', *Neuropsychol.*, vol. 4, pp. 49–64.

Albert, D. J. (1966b), 'Memory in mammals: evidence for a system involving nuclear ribonucleic acid', *Neuropsychol.*, vol. 4, pp. 79–92.

Allison, R. S. (1962), *The Senile Brain*, Arnold.

Barbizet, J. (1965), 'Lobe frontal et mémoire', *Annales Médico-Psychol.*, vol. 2, pp. 289–302.

Barondes, S. (1965), 'Relationship of biological regulatory mechanisms to learning and memory', *Nature*, vol. 205, pp. 18–21.

Bartlett, F. C. (1932), *Remembering*, Cambridge University Press.

Benton, A. (1955). *The Revised Visual Retention Test: Clinical and Experimental Applications*, State University of Iowa.

Bergson, H. (1911), *Matter and Memory*, Allen. (Originally published 1896)

Blakemore, C. B., and Falconer, M. A. (1967), 'Long-term effects of anterior temporal lobectomy on certain cognitive functions', *J. Neurol. Neurosurg. Psychiat.*, vol. 30, pp. 364–7.

Bleuler, E. (1924), *Textbook of Psychiatry*, New York, Macmillan.

Brodmann, K. (1902), 'Experimenteller und klinischer Beitrag zur Psychopathologie der polyneuritischen Psychose', *J. Psychol. Neurol.*, vol. 1, pp. 225–46.

Burnham, W. H. (1904), 'Retroactive amnesia: illustrative cases and a tentative explanation', *Amer. J. Psychol.*, vol. 14, pp. 118–32.

Cameron, D. E. (1940), 'Certain aspects of defect of recent memory occurring in psychoses of senium', *Arch. Neurol. Psychiat*, vol. 43, pp. 987–92.

Claparède, E. (1951) 'Recognition and me-ness', in D. Rapaport (ed.). *Organization and Pathology of Thought*, Columbia University Press. (Original paper published 1911)

Cohen, H. D., Barondes, S. H., and Ervin, F. R. (1966), 'Puromycin and cycloheximide: different effects on hippocampal electrical activity', *Science*, vol. 154, pp. 1557–8.

Cronholm, B., and Blomquist, C. (1959), 'Memory disturbances after electroconvulsive therapy. 2. Conditions one week after a series of treatments', *Acta psychiat. neurol. Scand.*, vol. 34, pp. 18–25.

Cronholm, B., and Molander, L. (1957), 'Memory disturbances after electroconvulsive therapy. 1. Conditions six hours after electric shock treatment', *Acta psychiat. neurol. Scand.*, vol. 32, pp. 280–306.

Cronholm, B., and Molander, L. (1964), 'Memory disturbances after electroconvulsive therapy. 5. Conditions one month after a series of treatments', *Acta psychiat. neurol. Scand.*, vol. 40, pp. 211–16.

Cronholm, B., and Ottoson, J.-O. (1963), 'Ultrabrief stimulus technique in electroconvulsive therapy', *J. nerv. ment. Dis.*, vol. 137, pp. 117–23.

Delay, J. (1942), *Les Dissolutions de la Mémoire*, Presses Universitaires de France.

Delboeuf, J. J. R. (1876), *Théorie Générale de la Sensibilité*, Brussels.

Dugas, L. (1931), *Les Maladies de la Mémoire et de l'Imagination*, Vrim.

Ebbinghaus, H. (1885), *Über das Gedächtnis*, Duncker. Translated as *Memory*, Dover, 1964.

Ey, H. (1950), 'Les troubles de la mémoire', *Études Psychiatriques*, no. 9, Desclee de Brouwer.

Eysenck, H. J. (1957), *The Dynamics of Anxiety and Hysteria*, Praeger.

Fisher, C. M., and Adams, R. D. (1964), 'Transient global amnesia', *Acta neurol. Scand.*, supp. 9, vol. 40.

Freud, S. (1929), *Inhibitions, Symptoms and Anxiety*, Hogarth. (First published, 1925)

Freud, S. (1953), *The Interpretation of Dreams*, Hogarth. (First published, 1900)

Freud, S. (1960), *The Psychopathology of Everyday Life*, Hogarth. (First published in German, 1900)

Freud. S, (1961), *Civilization and its Discontents*, Hogarth. (First published, 1930)

Garcia, J., and Ervin, F. R. (1967), 'Appetites, aversions, and addictions: a model for visceral memory', *Rec. Adv. Bio. Psychiat.*, vol. 10, Plenum Press.

Gombrich, E. (1960), *Art and Illusion*, Pantheon.

Graham, F. K., and Kendall, B. S. (1960), 'Memory-for-designs text: revised general manual', *Percept. motor Skills*, vol. 11, pp. 147–88.

Gregor, A. (1909), 'Beiträge zur Psychopathologie des Gedächtnisses', *Mschr. Psychiat. Neurol.*, vol. 25, pp. 218–55, 339–86.

Grünthal, E., and Störring, G. E. (1930a), 'Über das Verhalten umschriebener, völliger, Merkunfähigkeit', *Mschr. Psychiat. Neurol.*, vol. 74, pp. 254–69.

Grünthal, E., and Störring, G. E. (1930b), 'Erganzende Beobachtungen und Bemerkungen zu dem in Band 74', *Mschr. Psychiat. Neurol.*, vol. 77, pp. 374–82.

Grünthal, E., and Störring, G. E. (1956), 'Abschlieszende Stellungsnahme zu der vorstehenden Arbeit von H. Völkel und R. Stolze über den Fall B.', *Mschr. Psychiat. Neurol.*, vol. 132, pp. 309–11.

Head, H. (1920), *Studies in Neurology*, Oxford University Press.

Hebb, D. O. (1949), *The Organization of Behavior*, Wiley.

Hebb, D. O. (1961), 'Distinctive features of learning in the higher animals', in J. F. Delafresnaye (ed.), *Brain Mechanisms and Learning*, Blackwell.

Hopwood, J. S., and Snell, H. J. (1933), 'Amnesia in relation to crime', *J. ment. Sci.*, vol. 79, pp. 27–41.

Hulicka, I. M., and Grossman, J. L. (1967), 'Age-group comparisons for the use of mediators in paired-associate learning', *J. Gerontol.*, vol. 22, pp. 45–51.

Hunter, I. M. L. (1957), *Memory: Facts and Fallacies*, Penguin Books (rev. edn entitled *Memory*, 1964).

Hydén, H. (1965), 'Activation of nuclear R N A in neurons and glia in learning', in D. P. Kimble (ed.), *The Anatomy of Memory*, Science and Behavior Books.

Janet, P. (1920), *The Major Symptoms of Hysteria*. New York, Macmillan.

Janet, P. (1903), *Les Obsessions et la Psychasthénie*, Alcan.

Janet, P. (1942), Preface to J. Delay, *Les Dissolutions de la Mémoire*, Presses Universitaires de France.

John, E. R. (1965), 'The front-stoop approach to memory', *Perspect. Biol. Med.*, vol. 9, pp. 35–53.

Jung, C. G. (1953), 'The archetypes and the collective unconscious', *Collected Works*, vol. 9, Pantheon.

Jung, C. G., and Riklin, F. (1904), 'Diagnostische Assoziationstudien', *J. Psych. Neurol.*, vol. 3, pp. 193–215.

Koestler, A. (1964), *The Act of Creation*, New York, Macmillan.

Kraepelin, E. (1887), 'Über Erinnerungsfalschungen', *Arch. Psvchiat.*, vol. 17, pp. 830–43; vol. 18, pp. 199–239, 395–436.

Kral, V. A., and Durost, H. B. (1953), 'A comparative study of the amnesic syndrome in various organic conditions', *Amer. J. Psychiat.*, vol. 110, pp. 41–7.

Kral, V. A. (1957), *Types of Memory Dysfunction in Senescence*, Paper read at Confer. Amer. Psychiat. Assoc., Montreal, 8–9 November.

Kral, V. A. (1962), 'Senescent forgetfulness: benign and malignant', *Canadian med. Assoc. J.*, vol. 86, pp. 257–60.

Lehmann, J. (1954), *The Whispering Gallery*, Harcourt Brace.

McDougall, W. (1926), *Outline of Abnormal Psychology*, Scribner.

Melton, A. W. (1963), 'Implications of short-term memory for a general theory of memory', *J. verb. Learn. verb. Behav.*, vol. 2, pp. 1–21.

Meyer, V. (1959), 'Cognitive changes following temporal lobectomy for relief of temporal lobe epilepsy', *A.M.A. Arch. Neurol. Psychiat.*, vol. 81, pp. 299–309.

Miller, G. A., Galanter, E., and Pribram, K. H. (1960), *Plans and the Structure of Behavior*, Holt.

Milner, B. (1965), 'Memory disturbance after bilateral hippocampal lesions', in P. M. Milner and S. E. Glickman (eds.), *Cognitive Processes and the Brain*, Van Nostrand.

Nabokov, V. (1966), *Speak Memory*, Putnam.

Parfitt, D. N., and Gall, C. M. C. (1944), 'Psychogenic amnesia: the refusal to remember', *J. ment. Sci.*, vol. 90, pp. 511–31.

Paul, I. H. (1959), 'Studies in remembering', *Psychol. Issues*, vol. 1, no. 2, International University Press.

Pavlov, I. P. (1927), *Conditioned Reflexes*, Oxford University Press.

Penfield, W. (1954), 'Studies of the cerebral cortex of man – A review and an interpretation', in E. D. Adrian, F. Bremer,

H. H. Jasper (eds.), *Brain Mechanisms and Consciousness*, Blackwell.

Penfield, W., and Jasper, H. (1954), *Epilepsy and the Functional Anatomy of the Human Brain*, Little-Brown.

Penfield, W., and Milner, B. (1958), 'The memory deficit produced by bilateral lesions in the hippocampal zone', *Arch. Neurol. Psychiat.*, vol. 79, pp. 475–97.

Peterson, L. R., and Peterson, M. J. (1959), 'Short-term retention of individual verbal items', *J. exp. Psychol.*, vol. 58, pp. 193–8.

Pick, A. (1876), 'Zur Casuistik der Erinnerungsfälschungen', *Archiv. f. psych.*, vol. 6, pp. 568–74.

Posner, M. I., and Rossman, E. (1965), 'Effect of size and location of informational transforms upon short-term retention', *J. exp. Psychol.*, vol. 70, pp. 496–505.

Pribram, K. H. (1958), 'Comparative neurology and the evolution of behavior', in A. Roe and G. G. Simpson (eds.), *Behavior and Evolution*, Yale University Press.

Ranschburg, P. (1911), *Das kranke Gedächtnis*, Barth.

Ribot, T. A. (1882), *The Diseases of Memory*, Appleton.

Righetti, R. (1920), 'Contributo allo studio delle amnesie lacunari', *Riv. patol.*, vol. 25, pp. 261–84.

Rizzo, E. M. (1955), 'Sulla sindroma di Korsakoff', *Rassegna di Stud. Psychiat.*, vol. 44, pp. 800–16.

Ross, J. (1890), 'On the psychical disorders of peripheral neuritis', *J. ment. Sci.*, vol. 36, pp. 156–72.

Russell, W. R. (1959), *Brain, Memory, Learning*, Oxford University Press.

Russell, W. R., and Nathan, P. W. (1946), 'Traumatic amnesia', *Brain*, vol. 69, pp. 280–300.

Scheid, W. (1934), 'Zur Pathopsychologie des Korsakow-Syndroms', *Z. Neurol. Psychiat.*, vol. 151, pp. 246–369.

Shadbolt, M. (1965), *Among the Cinders*, Athenaeum.

Shepard, R. N. (1967), 'Recognition memory for words, sentences, and pictures', *J. verb. Learn. verb Behav.*, vol. 6, pp. 156–63.

Sherrington, C. S. (1906), *The Integrative Action of the Nervous System*, Scribner.

Skinner, B. F. (1938), *The Behavior of Organisms*, Appleton.

Somerville, C. W. (1931), 'Concussion and memory', *Tr. Med.-Chir. Soc. Edinburgh*, 1930–31, pp. 121–35.

Stengel, E. (1950), 'Intensive electro-convulsant therapy', *J. ment. Sci.*, vol. 97, p. 139.

Stern, W. (1938), *General Psychology*, New York, Macmillan.

Syz, H. (1937), 'Recovery from loss of mnemic retention after head trauma', *J. gen. Psychol.*, vol. 17, pp. 355–87.

Talland, G. A. (1965), *Deranged Memory*, Academic Press.

Talland, G. A., Sweet, W. H., and Ballantine, H. T. (1968), 'Amnesic syndrome with anterior communicating artery aneurysm', *J. nerv. ment. Dis.*, vol. 145, in press.

Underwood, B. J. (1949), *Experimental Psychology, an Introduction*, Appleton.

Underwood, B. J. (1957), 'Interference and forgetting', *Psychol. Rev.*, vol. 64, pp. 49–60.

Watson, J. B., and Rayner, R. (1920), 'Conditioned emotional reactions', *J. exp. Psychol.*, vol. 3, pp. 1–14.

Waugh, N. C., and Norman, D. A. (1965), 'Primary memory', *Psychol. Rev.*, vol. 72, pp. 89–104.

Weschler, D. A. (1945), 'A standardized memory scale for clinical use', *J. Psychol.*, vol. 19, pp. 87–95.

Welch, D. (1943), *Maiden Voyage*, Routledge and Kegan Paul (Penguin Books, 1954).

Williams, M. (1950), 'Memory studies in E.C.T.', *J. Neurol. Neurosurg. Psychiat.*, vol. 13, pp. 314–19.

Williams, M. (1953), 'Investigation of amnesic defects by progressive prompting', *J. Neurol. Neurosurg. Psychiat.*, vol. 16, pp. 14–18.

Williams, M. (1968), 'The measurement of memory in clinical practice', *Brit. J. soc. clin. Psychol.*, vol. 6, in press.

Williams, M., and Smith, H. (1954), 'Mental disturbances in tuberculous meningitis', *J. Neurol. Neurosurg. Psychiat.*, vol. 17, pp. 173–82.

Zangwill, O. L. (1943), 'Clinical tests of memory impairment', *Proc. Roy. Soc. Med.*, vol. 36, pp. 576–80.

Zangwill, O. L. (1950), 'Amnesia and the generic image', *Quart. J. exp. Psychol.*, vol. 2, pp. 7–12.

Zangwill, O. L., and Whitty, C. W. M. (1966), 'Traumatic amnesia', in C. W. M. Whitty and O. L. Zangwill (eds.), *Amnesia*, Butterworth.

Index